THE
TOUR DE
FRANCE

THE TOUR DE FRANCE

...TO THE BITTER END

EDITED BY RICHARD NELSSON

guardianbooks

Published by Guardian Books 2012

2 4 6 8 10 9 7 5 3

Copyright © Guardian News and Media Ltd 2012

First published in Great Britain in 2012 by
Guardian Books
Kings Place, 90 York Way
London N1 9GU

www.guardianbooks.co.uk

A CIP catalogue record for this book is
available from the British Library

ISBN 9780852653364

Text design by seagulls.net
Cover design by Two Associates
Printed and bound in Great Britain by CPI Group (UK) Ltd,
Croydon, CR0 4YY

CONTENTS

INTRODUCTION
MY TOUR DE FRANCE
William Fotheringham

The Tour de France and the *Guardian* have been intertwined for 30 years of my life and counting. The paper was part of my upbringing – within my family the tradition of reading it goes back to the 1950s – and, as a teenage cycling fan in the early 1980s, Geoff Nicholson and Charlie Burgess's reports were an integral part of summers spent devouring cycling magazines and training with a view to racing in France myself. Merely writing for the paper, however, let alone writing about the Tour in its pages, never entered my wildest dreams.

It is humbling for any incumbent to be given a reminder of the greats who have preceded him, and that, pretty much, was how I felt on looking at the pages that follow this. It is also hugely uplifting. I had been aware that the *Guardian* and *Observer*'s tradition of Tour writing was a strong and distinguished one, but this book is a reminder of the power and quality of the writers the two papers have employed over the years. There is much to treasure here: the late Chris Brasher with what was probably the definitive interview with Tom Simpson, another sorely missed great, Geoffrey Nicholson, on the enigmatic Sean Kelly, Charlie Burgess on Paul Sherwen and the life of a *domestique*. There are more familiar names to readers of recent years in Hugh McIlvanny, Frank Keating, Stephen Bierley, and Richard Williams. It is heartwarming to feel that although it is Europe that has produced the greatest cycling writing – Pierre Chany and Antoine Blondin in France, Gianni Brera and Dino Buzzati in Italy – this paper's writers can at least hold their own in their company.

The pieces in this book are a reminder that since the race's inception, the Tour and its writers have evolved continually, if gradually. I have witnessed that evolution at first hand. In 1994, before I began covering the race for the *Guardian*, with only five years in journalism behind me, I was briefed by the then *Guardian* Tourman, Stephen Bierley, and the sports editor at the time, Mike Averis, to whom my eternal thanks are due for having the nerve to entrust me with what turned out to a job spanning three decades, the 90s, the noughties and into the "tweenies".

The key thing to remember, they told me, was that on days when there was not much developing in the race overall, a day perhaps when the stage victory went to an obscurity of foreign origin who might not be of great interest to British readers, I should have no fear of writing what we hacks call "colour". In Tour terms, that means digressing far from the bare facts of the action into what might loosely be described as "Tourism" – evoking and explaining the cultural, social, scenic, gastronomic and political context that makes the race the unique event it is.

That thought now brings on a wry smile. The success of the British contingent in the Tour in recent years has changed the whole equation. The Tour has been transformed in the last 10 years into a highlight of the British sporting summer, where Mark Cavendish is expected to win all the flat stages, Wiggins is a favourite to win the thing overall, and a team sponsored by – cue wry smiles from all *Guardian* aficionados – Sky television and News Corp is at the heart of the action. There are no "quiet days" where an Italian or French journey-man – who might have been handpicked for his very obscurity, to paraphrase Nicholson – will hold centre stage: the four-week soap opera has British players at its very heart. The Tour is now as much a British story, with major British actors, as the Premiership, a Rugby World Cup, an Ashes Tour.

The first Tour I covered for the paper, 1994, can now be highlighted as a point when the race began to change for British fans. The dramatic victory in that year's prologue for Chris

Boardman marked the first time since 1962 that any Briton had led the Tour, and Boardman, having gained massive notoriety in winning the 4 km pursuit at the Barcelona Olympics two years earlier, was the first household name in British sport to wear the *maillot jaune*. A few days later, the depth of the passion for the race in Britain was dramatically shown in Le Tour en Angleterre, when the race visited Dover, Brighton and Portsmouth via a swathe of south-east England. Millions lined the roads, among them a youthful David Millar, who wore yellow himself in 2000.

The transformation can be traced seamlessly from the Boardman Tour. In the following four years, the "Professor" wore yellow three times. The Festina Tour of 1998, marred by the greatest drugs scandal the race has ever seen, turned the race into a breaking news event in its own right, and that was followed by the eruption of Lance Armstrong – like him or loathe him, no one can deny his influence – into the mainstream consciousness. The maelstrom of hype, controversy and success that whirled around the Texan held public interest up to the Tour start in London in 2007 – still hailed by the organisers as one of the race's greatest popular moments – the arrival of Cavendish and Wiggins in 2008–9, and Sky's emergence in 2010. The *Guardian* can be said to have played its part in the way the race and cycling in a broader sense has become part of the national consciousness, by being the only Fleet Street paper with a specialist cycling correspondent – which it still is today – and by sending that writer to the Tour, fully resourced. That commitment shines through in the fact that, as long ago as 2004, the *Observer* first hired Wiggins to produce ghosted columns, and he was joined by Cavendish in the *Guardian* in 2007 and 2008. "*Guardian* man wins Tour de France stage" made a great front page on July 10 2008, when Le Cav took his first Tour stage win in Chateauroux.

Until recently, the mission of a Tour correspondent was essentially explanatory. The Tour was a foreign competition which took place, in one's mind, where the readership went on holiday or liked to think they might do one day; the day's piece was also, critically since the arrival of Channel 4 television in 1986, an addendum to what the reader might well have seen the previous evening. Tactics needed to be presented in an accessible way; the minutiae of the sport explained – how the riders went to the toilet and precisely what a domestique did being the perennial favourites – and lexicons of French jargon such as *peloton*, *lanterne rouge*, and *musette* compiled. That was a subtle variation on Simpson and Nicholson's day, when the Tour was more removed: 24 hours travel away from Britain and many of the readership might have fought on French soil or knew someone who had. (On which note, the 1943 piece from Garry Hogg is a gem, pure and simple.) Nowadays, the Tour writer is producing copy for a far broader and far more knowledgeable audience, whose knowledge is fuelled by the internet, a brace of fat, glossy British magazines, extensive coverage of cycling virtually year round on Eurosport. The readership now is a broad church, and I suspect many of them ride bikes a good deal as well as reading about the racing.

So you are still a newspaperman on the Tour, but the paper is no longer the core activity. Comment on a major event is instant via Twitter – but still has to be carefully thought out – much of the audience we are now writing for will read the report within minutes of its being written, as soon as it goes on the paper's website, and feedback is almost simultaneous. Corrections now are as likely to stem from a well-informed fan or blogger questioning a fact or an assumption, as from the subeditors who, in my early days, would lend the authority of a university High Table to debate over the spelling of Abdoujaparov or the capitals on his nickname – the coining of which remains one of my proudest Tour achievements – the Tashkent Terror. By 2011, the social media circle was completed when one day's intro was inspired by an exchange with a fan on Twitter. (For the record it was a piece about

Edvald Boasson Hagen's stage win in Lisieux and Baked Alaska pudding).

There have been other changes. In 1995, the sole Briton – of British birth at least – remaining in the race in the final half was Sean Yates, probably the most popular racer these shores have ever produced. Yates was in his final Tour, suffering from injury, and, as his Tour ground towards the end, his abandon imminent, I wanted to find out how he was. He was on the other side of his team car, and as I edged round the car to find him, he edged in his turn round to the other side. I snuck gently round again, he snuck in his turn to the opposite, never catching my eye. Eventually, I caught him up, to be greeted with the words, "Can't you just f***ing stop chasing me!", or something of that ilk. Nowadays, such a scene is barely imaginable. Yates would be immured in a team bus, and I would ask a press officer about his sore shin.

The Tour is more demanding for a writer now, more diffuse, more competitive, more remote, but at the same time impossible to escape at any time of day. The Festina drugs scandal of 1998 was an abrupt introduction to the idea that on the Tour, breaking news could happen outside press room opening hours. Suddenly, events developed up to the final edition deadline at roughly 1am French time. The internet has made the news cycle virtually 24 hours now. Dinner, much loved of Tour correspondents down the years, was once sacrosanct as the time when the day's action was chewed over at genteel length, but no more. The more delectable the evening's chosen starter and the more vintage the Burgundy airing on the table, the more likely it was that you would be interrupted by the news of a positive test or a police raid on a team hotel.

The great myth in the *Guardian* sports desk used to be that the Tour writer would drive down the race route without a care in the world each day looking for a relaxed lunch. The first part was true, the second sadly not. Driving the day's stage route was a habit I picked up from Nicholson and Bierley; actually seeing the little hills and villages where the riders would be racing, reading the placards held up by the fans, checking the architecture and flora, would all provide "colour", if it were needed. It goes against my personal grain, but the practice is now officially discouraged due to a spate of accidents involving spectators and race vehicles. Now, it's a thrash down the motorway, a sandwich from a service station, and find your "colour" elsewhere.

There are other changes. The traffic jams are grimmer, as more people come to the race and the roads around the race are busier in themselves. The Tour is less exclusively French, more cosmopolitan. The lingua franca of the peloton, the default option within most teams, is English rather than French; so too the press room, where the second choice for translation is English. The race is more eventful, more dramatic, with barely a day going by without a major crash or controversy. That's due in part to the fact that while from its inception the race had always been run by newspapermen, today's organiser, Christian Prudhomme, is the first to have cut his teeth in television. His routes are more inventively designed, more experimental, to facilitate daily drama. The great joy of today's Tour is that it is far less predictable than in the past.

Part of that is due to the fact that cycling's elephant in the room is now clearly visible. Drugs were an unspoken given in the early 1990s, rarely mentioned but constantly at the back of the mind; since 1998, the great challenge lies in working out the significance and implications of each positive test or a police inquiry. Since the Floyd Landis Tour of 2006, the race does not finish – in the writer's mind at least – when the yellow jersey crosses the line on the Champs-Élysées, but when the last urine test is pronounced clean. A positive for the winner, as in 2006 and 2010, can extend the race by years, through a long series of legal challenges and appeals.

Fortunately, the elements that make the Tour great will never go away. The sporting soap opera will always have its different daily backdrop. France may change but the backdrop of La France Profonde remains essentially the same. The great theatres of the Tour – the Galibier, the Izoard, the Tourmalet, Simpson's Ventoux – are immutable. Bastille Day will always provide great amusement as the French cyclists' desperation to win on their national holiday seems to exponentially reduce their capacity to cross the line first. Spectator groups come and go, depending on which nation is in the van, but the gloomy looking Belgians in the camper van flying a Belgian tricolour bearing an obscure pun on the emblem of Flanders, a lion, and the former Belgian champion Claude Criquielion, still park up somewhere along the route, although Cri-Cri retired in the year of my first Tour, 1990.

The Tour has always been a challenge for reporters. The first ones rode with the riders. Later, they drove open-top cars among the peloton, fraternising with the men they wrote about. Before television, they had to imagine much of what went on; before WIFI, the challenge of merely getting the words to where they needed to be should not be understated. The Tour's hacks have had to come to terms with fatigue, boredom, chauvinism, lousy telephone lines, traffic queues and, inevitably, officialdom.

At least once, on any given Tour, you will be driving towards the day's stage start or finish in a car bearing the magic *laissez-passer* on the windscreen, the access-all-areas badge that lets you into the Tour's restricted zone, when you encounter a gendarme with a stern look on his face. You cannot pass, he insists, the road is closed to traffic. But I have a Tour sticker, I am with the Tour, you reply, pointing to the green or yellow band on the windscreen. He is implacable: You cannot pass, the road is closed to traffic. You remain insistent: but I have a Tour sticker … Maddening the first time, funny by the 10th, and while it may be bad for the blood pressure, there is a curious comfort in the thought that the French uniformed mind is likely to ensure that whoever is covering the Tour for the Guardian in the 2020s will have the same experience. If he or she gets as much enjoyment, adrenalin, and job satisfaction as I have – and I suspect my predecessors enjoyed as well – they will be lucky indeed.

William Fotheringham has covered the Tour de France for the *Guardian* since 1994; his latest book, *Eddy Merckx: Half Man Half Bike*, was the first cycling book to top the Sunday Times bestseller lists. He can be contacted via twitter @willfoth or his website www.williamfotheringham.com

CHAPTER ONE
THE BEGINNING

PARIS WEEK BY WEEK

THE GREAT BICYCLE RACE

ARMY OF PRESSMEN AND PHOTOGRAPHERS

COURSE OF 2,760 MILES

LOCAL ENTHUSIASTS

From Our Own Correspondent

PARIS, Saturday

The political and financial crisis through which the country is passing would appear to interest the average newspaper reader far less than the Tour de France, if one may judge by the much greater amount of space given to the latter. The Tour de France is a bicycle race, open to competitors of all nationalities, over a course which varies slightly from year to year, but more or less follows a sort of outer circle of French territory. The total distance this year is 2,760 miles, divided into laps which will make the race, which started from Paris on Wednesday, finish in Paris again twenty-four days later. The two leading places are at present occupied by two citizens of Luxembourg, but there is plenty of time for them to be displaced by the Belgians, Dutchmen, Germans, or Italians, who are among the competitors, to say nothing of the Frenchmen. Not only are the roads lined everywhere by local enthusiasts, but the competitors are followed, and often impeded, by a whole army of sympathising bicyclists, as well as by supporters, pressmen and officials of the course in motor cars, and even by a travelling repair shop. Some papers charter aeroplanes from which to watch and photograph the race. The whole of this caravan, after striking up from Paris to Lille, hugging the Belgian frontier and touching at Metz, in Lorraine, but not going any nearer to Germany, will now skirt Switzerland, cut across the moun-

letter which he has written, in the same way as a certain royal Eton boy who wrote to Queen Victoria, his grandmother, to ask for pocket money, and immediately sold her letter of refusal to a collector.

The Tourist Traffic

The tourist industry is so important in France, and the "invisible exports" represented by the money spent in the country by foreign tourists contribute so materially to its commercial balance, that it is not surprising that the Government has decided to organise a course of training and an examination for young men and women who hope to obtain employment in connection with tourist planning and propaganda. Passing the examination will secure a diploma, which will be a certificate of competence as a "Collaborateur du Tourisme." The examination covers at least one and, if possible, two foreign languages, and the candidate will be expected to show, in conversation, that he or she is capable of giving information about travel facilities and sight-seeing opportunities in France generally, and also in greater detail in a particular district chosen and studied. The main test, however, is the draft presentation of a handbook about the chosen district, and the means of access to it. This draft must include one chapter fully written. The candidate must also know something about hotels and their prices, about spas and their healing properties, about facilities for tennis and golf, and about "gastronomy," with special reference to the best local dishes.

Theatrical Storm in a Teacup

There has arisen this week one of those storms in the theatrical teacup in which Paris delights. It was about the awards to the theatrical competitors at the Conservatoire in the class of comedy. The audience at the competition, which is held in public, did not hesitate to express its displeasure at the announcement that there would be no first prize either for men or women. As this audience, which is present by invitation, consists almost entirely of relatives and friends of the competitors, its disappointment was not in itself surprising; but it transpired that there had been trouble over the composition of the jury—they would be called the judges in England—and this was more serious, as it involved the absence of any representative of the Comédie-Française, and the prizewinners at the Conservatoire

CYCLING NOTES

The Manchester Guardian, 9 March 1903

A new race, "Le Tour de France", is to be started in June. It is to be run in six stages on consecutive Sundays, as follows: Paris to Lyons (500 kilometres), Lyons to Marseilles (350 kilometres), Marseilles to Toulouse (300 kilometres), Toulouse to Bordeaux (250 kilometres), Bordeaux to Nantes (400 kilometres), and Nantes to Paris (400 kilometres). The first prizes will be 2,000, 1,200, 1,000, 800, 1,500, and 2,000 francs respectively, while 1,500, francs will be given to the rider who does the best aggregate time.

THE "TOUR DE FRANCE"

The Manchester Guardian, 21 February 1905

The 3,000-kilometre contest, known as the Tour de France, will be held on the 9th, 11th, 14th, 16th, 18th, 20th, 23rd, 25th, 27th, 29th, and 30th of July. The first prize is 4,000 francs and there are several other prizes, as well as prizes for the winners of each stage.

THE TURN OF THE WHEEL

by William Bolitho

The Manchester Guardian, 21 August 1924

Once upon a time there was an honest young mason who had three young children and a wife whom he adored. Now it came about that in one month, without speculation or luck, by his own hands and legs he won his fortune and bought the biggest house in the village where he will live happily ever afterwards. This is one of the twenty favourite themes of modern folk-lore; its catchword is "quick and honest riches"; its latest setting the 1924 Tour de France, or the story of Ottavio Bottecchia, champion cyclist.

In that wide stretch of Europe inhabited by short-headed, black-eyed, energetic men who lose their tempers and talk with their hands, a region roughly corresponding to France, Switzerland Walloon, Belgium, Italy and Bavaria, this Tour de France is the living Iliad. It comes about yearly. Two hundred of the toughest professional cyclists from these countries start from Paris for a 5,418-kilometre race round the borders of France – almost exactly the distance that separates Paris from Baghdad. It takes them a month, the whole of baking July, in fifteen stages. The first prize amounts to 60,000 francs, enough even nowadays to make a workman a man of fortune. It is the best-paid and best-known road race in that most modern and most democratic sport. Henri Desgranges, one of the personalities of France, owner of a daily sporting paper, the man who translated sport to France thirty years ago, invented it. Every year he stiffens its conditions, hardens its regulations, and by meditation on the geography of its route makes its hell for human endurance harder. It is the only way in which a man who cannot read or write can earn a fortune in a month without gambling, except with his neck.

Naturally it skirts throughout its length the extreme frontiers of human possibility. France is politically celebrated for her uncommon share of natural frontiers: the mountains of the Pyrenees on the south, the mountains of the Alps on her middle east. The road of the Tour follows these asperities with devilish exactness. The claimants for the quick fortune are strong men. In most years only a fourth of them finish the course, and they go to bed for a fortnight.

Bottecchia is a young mason from Frioul in Italy. He fits the legend of the poor young man who loves his family exactly; for the rest, he hates the bicycle, thinks of nothing else but his home. He cares nothing for honour, has no ambitions but that best house in the village, never smiles, never talks, and all the other professionals hate him. He is long and thin, with a nose like pick-axe. Last year he appeared for the first time and won second place. As soon as he was well, on the money he had gained he went into diligent training for the big prize again. His rivals in Italy, particularly Brunero, after discussing the oaf and the upstart with their national talent for criticism, put him out of their minds and wiped out the memory of his snatched win in their lesser triumphs on the track, on the road, throughout the year. Bottecchia helped them to forget by keeping on training for the Tour de France in strict seclusion.

At the start in Paris for this year's Tour Bottecchia met three chief enemies: Brunero, the legitimate idol of Italy, the reigning king of the road, who was out to win for ambition; the Pélissier brothers, the glory of France, who had a duty to their fellow-countrymen; Alavoine from Versailles, a giant who is older than he was, who must show us all that he is immune from age. Besides these, 180 others – young hopes feverish for fame. They started at three o'clock in the morning with 30,000 to see them off.

On this Tour de France the start is always given in the small hours of the morning to give the cyclists a chance to get away. If there was a more uncomfortable hour than that before dawn Desgranges would choose it. For the whole run is done, with hardly a break, between two lines of spectators ranged round the border of France like an ornamental edge of applause and curiosity. In the wildest parts of Brittany and Savoy there is never a kilometre without a waiting car or motor-cycle. In the big towns on the evening of arrival they mobilise regiments of police to keep a streak of road open to the control table. The book of rules for the racers has 200 pages, each a guard against fraud or violence that the cunning of these 180, mad to win by any means, may devise. Each competitor, says the first article, must race as if he were alone on a lonely road – mend his own tyres, drink out of his own bottle, sponge the blood out of his eyes in a fall, or bandage a broken leg as best he may without the slightest assistance from competitor or follower until he arrives at the end of his stage.

The course turned into dolorous allegory. First, Pélissier the Great, last year's victor, who began the Tour ("this job for convicts" he called it) because of "patriotic duty to his fellow-countrymen", being their incomparably best racer, abandoned the contest in Normandy. He fell into dispute with Desgranges as to whether the supplementary jersey he threw into a ditch en route counted as "tools", and so on no account to be got rid of between stopping-places. Alavoine, who was racing for a different sort of pride, the old hero, fell to twentieth rank at the Pyrenees. For the first week the lonely shingled paths of Brittany, past dour Stations of the Cross and innumerable exiled churches, then past the 300-mile stretch of sand and flint that descends down the Atlantic side. Then come, in the Basque country, the Justices of the Peace, those calm, inhuman shoulders of the great Pyrenean range: Aubisque, Tourmalet, Aspin, which no car can climb without resting to cool, which separate and inexorably classify the racers. Until then these cling together, saving their forces for this Pyrenean climb, the hardest test humanity has invented for the ultimate strength of legs. Bottecchia had been thinking of these giants in silence since Paris. On their shoulders he won the race. Without once stopping, hardly checking speed, putting up the record for the stage, he forced Aubisque, Tourmalet and the rest and drew up in Luçon, his face a grimacing mask of fatigue, a good hour in front of Brunero and Mottiat. Huot and Buysse, daring youngsters, had kept him company farthest – halfway up the first ascent. Brunero, the man who raced for glory, had been inexorably parted from the man who raced for home by the great knuckles of the mountain. He arrived bruised, collapsing, as silent for once as his butt Bottecchia. Half of the rest limped back to country railway stations to take the train for Paris.

The rest of the race – the dust of the Midi, where crowds out of human memory blocked the roads and brought dozens to bloody spill, the terrible 10-mile rise of the Crau, near Nice, the heart-breaking asperities of the Savoy and the Lower

Alps, where the villages in the distance seem like painted toys, past old streets of folk-lore roofs in Alsace, to the black slag-cemented roads in the North Country – was the history of Brunero's chase to catch up: ambition against home-seeking. And the stronger won. Bottecchia had beaten Alavoine, he had outlasted Pélissier; at Strasbourg his last determined rival, Brunero, gave up. The young mason of Frioul entered Paris a conqueror. A delirium of flowers and voices waited for him; best of all, the envelope with the cheque. The people, those strata too near the fundamental needs of life to taste any of the refined virtue of amateurism, understand Bottecchia, the professional of professionals, who only fought for money. For them the acted legend has the end they most approve.

PARIS WEEK BY WEEK

by Our own correspondent
The Observer, 27 June 1930

Once more the whole of the French working class is passion-ately interested in the "Tour de France", the bicycle race over the whole outer circuit of the roads of the country, and once more dense crowds have turned out to watch the start of the walking race from Paris to Strasbourg. The undimin-ished enthusiasm for these two events shows that the sort of athletic prowess which the average Frenchman really admires is not a matter of games, but of endurance. This volatile, vivacious, loquacious, and nervous race instinctively respects the man who can doggedly endure to the bitter end. It is a most curious illustration of national psychology, but there can be no question of the truth. The Frenchman may despise a man who is not quick. He may delight in himself being supple and adaptable in finding short cuts and turning difficulties; but he reserves his loudest cheers for persistence.

TOUR DE FRANCE RESULT

The Manchester Guardian, 28 July 1930

The cycle race round France was won to-day by the Frenchman Leducq, whose time for the 4,818 kilometres was 172 hr 12min 22sec. The race consisted of 21 stages.

GAMES AND PLAYERS: THE TOUR DE FRANCE

The Manchester Guardian, 14 July 1931

France is not much stirred this year by the cycling race of 3,200 miles round the country. The event, which is ridden in 24 stages, began on June 30, and will end on July 26. It has been held annually for about 30 years, and on some occasions has been the country's chief topic of conversation for a month. This year the entry – about 90 riders – was smaller. Many famous names are missing, and, according to some Paris newspapers, there appeared in the early stages to be a tacit agreement among competitors not to hurry matters. One rider was disqualified for being towed several miles by a motor-lorry, but this is a form of comic relief which enlivens the Tour de France every year.

It must be admitted that the race is a very grim business through the stages that traverse the Pyrenees and the French Alps. Here the ordeal seems to be out of all proportion to the prizes these professional riders receive. Snow, mist, and mud on the high roads, narrow, stone-covered tracks, terrible climbing, and dangerous descents are the lot of competitors on three of the stages. Discouraged by punctures at crucial moments, riders have been known to throw away their machines. H. Opperman, an Australian, was tenth of the 64 survivors at the end of the ninth stage, and A. Magne, a Frenchman, was leading. Six countries are represented.

EUROPEAN CYCLE RACING

The Manchester Guardian, 20 June 1933

Six Continental countries have this summer arranged cycle races along almost the whole length of their frontiers or coasts. The chief event is the race of 2,700 miles around France, which will begin on June 27. Public enthusiasm over these races puzzles British observers. Foreigners by the hundred will admit that rarely is a great tour completed without several cases of advantages gained by arrangement between competitors. Rich prizes go to the winners. A victor in a recent 1,800-mile race netted nearly £2,000 for his pains. And pains there undoubtedly are, for the mountain stages are terrible ordeals. The races are financed chiefly by cycle manufacturers who sponsor riders for publicity purposes. The cycle industry is extremely prosperous in some European countries; in France it is estimated that there is a machine to every six of the population.

STAMPEDE TO SEE CYCLING RACE

The Manchester Guardian, 22 July 1933

Twenty-eight people were injured – one is not expected to recover – when a crowd of about 10,000 got out of control here while awaiting the arrival of the competitors in the Tour de France, the round-France bicycle race. The crowd grew impatient and stormed the gates of the cycling stadium. Several policemen were knocked down in the rush. About a dozen people were taken to hospital.

GREAT CYCLING RACE: HOW PARIS SAW THE FINISH

The Manchester Guardian, 24 July 1933

Undeterred by the blazing sun, many thousands of people thronged the Parc des Princes, on the outskirts of Paris, this afternoon to see the finish of the Tour de France, the greatest cycle race of the year – and by far the most popular event in the sporting life of the French. The "better-class" people in France may look down on cycle-racing as a low and plebeian sport, and attach far more importance to the Davis Cup tournaments, but in the eyes of the populace Speicher, a mechanic from Pantin, the Paris suburb, who has just won the Tour de France, is much more of a national hero than any possible French winner of the Davis Cup.

During the past 24 days the "giants of the road" were the talk of every village and working-class café, and the yellow pullover worn by the cyclist with the highest score was a symbol of physical valour and national fame. Lately, even the weather was discussed chiefly in connection with the Tour de France. It was 86 in the shade in the South of France – would Archambaud stand the heat while in the Pyrenees? Weather, sunstroke, and the yellow pullover were mentioned in one breath.

JOURNALISTIC FERVOUR

During the past 24 days the great cycling race was the biggest feature in popular journalism. Each of the Paris evening papers had five or six "special correspondents" following the cyclists by car, whole pages giving humorous, descriptive, and technical articles every night, and, with photographs and giant headlines across the front page, continued day after day to inform the readers of the progress of the race of the "climatic conditions", and of the jubilant receptions given to the cyclists at the end of each stage. One paper had even an aeroplane to accompany the cyclists and to photograph them from above.

The collapse of Charles Pélissier, one of the French "aces", on the fifth day of the race was almost a subject of national mourning. Special correspondents were dispatched to the hospital to inquire after "Chariot's" sprained ankle and to describe in lyrical and dramatic terms the "tears in his eyes".

There were 80 starters, of whom 40 constituted the five national teams of eight "aces" each (France, Switzerland, Italy, Germany, and Belgium). The other 40 were the "isolated" cyclists not belonging to any team. It was a particularly good year for the French team; for out of the eight French "aces" seven finished the Tour de France. The Belgian team lost three on the way, the Swiss team three, the German team five, and the Italian team five. Out of the 80 starters 37 covered the whole distance.

THE PRIZES

The winner of the Tour de France received a prize of about £300, but the total of the prizes – including prizes for the separate stages, for final sprints at each stage, for the more difficult mountain climbs, and so on – came to nearly £10,000. The greatest benefits of all were reaped by the sporting and evening papers, whose circulation must have gone up by several hundred thousand in the past three weeks.

And now that the Tour de France is over the "dead season" has extended even to the realm of popular sport, and the sporting youth of plebeian France can now follow their "betters" and go on holiday with an easy mind. The Tour de France is the last survivor of the Paris season, and on August 1 "everybody" will be away. Many of the Paris shopkeepers – for France is a country where even shopkeepers take a holiday – are already preparing to lock up their doors and to hang up their notices: "Annual closing. To be reopened on September 15."

24 DAYS' CYCLE RACE

The Manchester Guardian, 29 July 1935

Romain Maes, a 22-year-old Belgian, won the marathon Tour de France cycle race which ended here to-day after lasting 24 days. Belgium was also placed first in the team event. Of the 93 competitors who left Paris on July 4 on their journey of nearly 1,500 miles, only 46 finished. During the course of the race one Spanish rider died in hospital from injuries sustained in a crash. A Frenchman is in hospital with a fractured skull and a number of other competitors were compelled to retire with minor injuries.

TOUR DE FRANCE WON BY BELGIAN – FRENCH RIDERS HOOTED

From a Paris Correspondent
The Manchester Guardian, 30 July 1935

Romain Maes, a fragile-looking Belgian who won the 2,700-mile cycling Tour de France, which began in Paris on July 4 and ended there on Sunday, expects his success to bring him £3,000. This will include contracts for track appearances in addition to his part of about £8,000 prize money shared among the 93 starters, 47 of whom finished. His chances were not considered rosy, but after winning the first of the

21 stages and finding himself wearer of the yellow jersey that distinguishes the leader from the riders, he brought such courage, tactical skill, and self-discipline to support riding ability that he carried the envied jersey throughout. It is typical of Maes that while earning plenty of money during the race, he did his own washing of socks and shorts. He and the members of the Belgian team who "nursed" him and contributed largely to his victory lived like Spartans throughout the race. Maes's average speed was a shade under 19 miles an hour.

The Belgians, who had four riders among the first six, easily won the international competition in which France, Germany, Spain and Italy finished after them in that order. The Frenchmen lost all inspiration when Antonin Magne, their leader and winner of last year's tour, was hurt by one of the hundreds of motor-cars that followed the riders, and had to retire. One death and several injuries were due to escorting cars, some of whose drivers were greeted by spectators with cries of "Assassins!" Hooting and derisive whistling greeted the French team at Nantes on account of their disappointing riding. Italy's team of eight starters was reduced to two, so that Morelli, an Italian who finished second and rode brilliantly over the terrible roads of the Pyrenees, had scarcely any support against the Belgian coalition. Dozens of penalties were inflicted for trickery – hanging on to cars, seeking pacing help, soliciting spectators for push up a hill, and so on – but despite that and murmurs of trafficking for stage placings and prizes, sporting France was almost unanimously behind the event.

THE GREAT BICYCLE RACE: ARMY OF PRESSMEN AND PHOTOGRAPHERS

From our own correspondent, Paris
The Observer, 4 July 1937

The political and financial crisis through which the country is passing would appear to interest the average newspaper reader far less than the Tour de France, if one may judge by the much greater amount of space given to the latter. The Tour de France is a bicycle race open to competitors of all nationalities, over a course which varies slightly from year to year, but more or less follows a sort of outer circle of French territory. The total distance this year is 2,760 miles, divided into laps which will make the race, which started from Paris on Wednesday, finish in Paris again 24 days later. The two leading places are at present occupied by two citizens of Luxembourg, but there is plenty of time for them to be displaced by the Belgians, Dutchmen, Germans, or Italians, who are among the competitors, to say nothing of the Frenchmen. Not only are the roads lined everywhere by local enthusiasts, but the competitors are followed, and often impeded, by a whole army of sympathising bicyclists, as well as by supporters, pressmen and officials of the course in motor cars, and even by a travelling repair shop.

Some papers charter aeroplanes from which to watch and photograph the race. The whole of this caravan, after striking up from Paris to Lille, hugging the Belgian frontier and touching at Metz, in Lorraine, but not going any nearer to Germany, will now skirt Switzerland, cut across the mountains to Nice, follow the Mediterranean coast, the Pyrenees, and the Bay of Biscay to Brittany and Normandy, before returning to Paris from Caen.

A MIRACULOUS RECOVERY

The Manchester Guardian, 19 July 1938

When a former world champion road cyclist made a miraculous recovery in one of the mountain stages of the race round France, which ends on July 31, he received many congratulations. From a place hopelessly among the laggards he flashed up hill and down dale till he was able to finish not far behind the leader. Asked how he had done it, he modestly replied that he hardly knew. It appeared that a sudden heaven-sent acquisition of form had enabled him to confound his rivals. An explanation was later supplied by judges of the race and a photographer. The rider was seen on several occasions hanging on to a motor-car, and an inglorious snapshot showing him "in the act" was published throughout France the following morning. "I had written an article in his praise," says a Paris commentator, "but I now call him a trickster, surprised with a pillager's hands upon a cup." This competitor, one of the greatest cyclists France has produced and a former winner of the Tour de France, was suspended from the race when the evidence was heard. After the first terrible ordeal over mountain roads, where for as much as nine miles there was not a yard of flat, Vervaecke, a Belgian, was leading with Bartali (Italy) second, and Goaxmat (France) third.

TOUR DE FRANCE

by Garry Hogg

The Manchester Guardian, 9 July 1943

I shall stick no more black-knobbed pins into my map of France. Till recently I had felt some satisfaction in doing so. The Ruhr was already full of them – pins that had been used in the First World War to indicate advances and salients in the near-static warfare of Flanders, now used to mark industrial sites bombed by our aircraft. When Abbeville was attacked, and Le Creusot, I had not felt it personally, for they were remote from the parts of France I once tried to make my own. But now event and memory have come too close to one another, and all because of a little village in Normandy with the improbable name of Vingt-Hanaps.

Searching my large-scale map to identify some recent targets of the Anglo-American bombers, I encountered the unexpected name: Vingt-Hanaps. "Twenty Goblets": by what odd freak of fancy was it so named? True, the village lies in the heart of cider-making country. In Vingt-Hanaps, moreover, lived my old friend Georges Enjalbert.

Over my wall map hangs a calendar, and perhaps it was because I looked up from the name to the date, July 1, that the little pieces of the picture slipped into position and suddenly Georges Enjalbert was beside me, for July was his great month, the month of the famous Tour de France. I had in those days a cycle with a tricoaster hub. Such things had not been seen in France. As I rode into Vingt-Hanaps, northward bound for Caen and the Channel Coast, something in its intricate mechanism failed. A short stocky man, with heavy black brows and swarthy skin, contemplated me in silence as I stood outside his smithy helpless. "Qu'y a-t-il, m'sieur?" he asked me civilly as looked up. In his hand, held like a toy, was a large hammer. I explained in laborious French, and within an hour a miracle had been wrought. I sat on a stool outside his smithy and watched him as he worked and talked. He must have been born a mechanic. His passion was long-distance cycling.

Together we turned the pages of old copies of *Le Miroir des Sports* as we drank the good *cidre du pays*. His great finger lay across a crowded photograph. There he was in his heyday among the aces at the start of the annual race round the French borders, nearly 3,000 miles to be covered in 20 days' cycling, with enforced rests on six days only. Forty-odd competitors – Belgian, Italian – and Georges Enjalbert among them. Georges Enjalbert clocking in at a control-point, being hosed by enthusiastic supporters as he sped by, racing at breakneck speed down precipitous slopes, pedalling apparently as fast (such is the resourcefulness of your sports cameraman) up equally precipitous hills, being forcibly fed and watered en route, and finally riding victoriously round the Paris Vélodrome with a garland about his shoulders that made all the leis of Hawaii look like buttonholes.

In May and June, as work slackened, Georges took more and more time off from the smithy. His cycle claimed him. I remember the first time I saw him in cycling rig. Gone were the heavy cord breeches, the leather apron, and stained shirt.

A bright yellow-and-black *maillot* was stretched taut about his great chest. Silk tights fitted his haunches like a pale-blue skin. From them bulged his great thighs – true cyclist's thighs, massive and corded, tapering into slim calves and neat ankles.

This Tour de France, I learnt from him, was a trial of almost fantastic dimensions. Westwards from Paris to Caen, a 150-mile starting lap; thence to Rennes and the interminable flat miles of Les Landes on the Biscay shore. A lap of 200 miles through the Pyrenees over slopes and saddlebacks that I had found tough even for walking – and no cyclist competing in the Tour de France has been known to demean himself by dismounting. Marseilles, Nice: the sun is formidable enough there in July even for someone who has nothing to do but lie and sip iced drinks. Yet still these lonely figures race on, widely separated now, looking desperately tired on their tiny, brilliantly coloured machines, but pedalling all day at 20 miles an hour, a speed which for most of us would be impossible for more than few minutes. Nor does their speed appreciably lessen among the hundreds of miles of the Juras, Alps and Vosges which they must next traverse.

July, then, is Georges Enjalbert's month. Were it not for the war even now he would be speeding, as a tourist-routier, since he is too old to compete among the aces, round this boundary of France. About his shoulders would be looped in figure-of-eight the slender spare tyre, on his gleaming handle-bars his twin canisters of refreshment, on his face that look of implacable determination that I used to see towards the end of his practice runs in May and June.

War has changed all that. Along the Grandes Routes Nationales the German legions march and countermarch behind their vaunted Atlantic Wall. Are they, I wonder, sometimes mysteriously impelled to draw aside, feeling the presence of ghostly figures speeding westwards on ghostly machines, league after arduous league? Is their night of hatred and mistrust crowded with yellow-and-black *maillots*, like that Georges Enjalbert, within which beat stout hearts, the hearts of men awaiting the signal to drive the grey-clad soldiers from their land? I like to think so. And I like to think that when the Atlantic Wall has crumbled, the coastal road will feel once more those spinning, silent tyres in a resurrected Tour de France.

CHAPTER TWO
"NORMALCY"

SEVEN DAYS OF SPORT

L'EQUIPE

*Le Dissez and the Irishman Elliott in trouble during the first
stage of this year's Tour de France*

The Hot Pursuit

Compiled by NORRIS McWHIRTER

A FEW seconds after the start of the 1959 Tour de France in Mulhouse on Thursday, the mammoth switchboard at the headquarters of the Paris information service, S.V.P., had glowed red, and 1,200 telephonists had begun working feverishly to assuage the thirst for information on the 2,706-mile-long, 24-day race anti-clock-wise round France.

To-day the 120 riders, with their massive entourage of managers, masseurs, wives and others, will sweep through the 142.9-mile Arras-Amiens section on their way to the Parc des Princes in Paris, which will be reached via the Pyrenees and the Alps on July 18.

Teams are entered from Holland, Luxembourg, Belgium, Italy, France, Spain, Switzerland and Germany. Individuals are also there from Portugal, Poland, Austria and Denmark together with four Englishmen, John Andrews, 25, Tony Hewson, 28, Brian Robinson, 29 (5th Tour) and Victor Sutton, 26; and the lone Irishman, Shay Elliott. Last year's winner, a Luxembourgeois, Charly Gaul, carries the hopes and even prayers of his 320,000 countrymen, while the French heroes are Jacques Anquetil,

Huttungen, 29, ran the fastest 5,000 metres in the world this year with 13 min. 51.8 sec.

DIVING.—Bruce Harlan, winner of the 1948 Olympic spring board title, was killed on Tuesday. He slipped from the high board in the University of Michigan bath, by great mischance struck the side of the bath, and died shortly after reaching hospital.

MOTOR RACING.—The 1959 Le Mans will be remembered for mechanical rather than human fatalities. The most significant record was the all-time low of 13 cars finishing from 54 starters.

When, with nearly four hours to go, the defending champions Phil Hill (United States) and Olivier Gendebien (Belgium) lost their overheated red Ferrari three laps in the lead, interest cooled. The Texan, Carroll Shelby, and the dashing Roy Salvadori, three laps in arrears, ground on to give Aston Martin their first victory with 2,701 miles (average 112.57 m.p.h.).

SOCCER.—A "low cultural level" was attributed to Soviet footballers in the June 21 edition of *Komsomolskaya Pravda*. The paper called for players who used their elbows, fists and violent language to be "cor-

RIDING ROUND THE CRISES

by DW Brogan, Clermont

The Observer, 6 July 1947

When I saw the young priest gazing intently at a notice in the window of the local Communist bookshop and propaganda centre, I was led to rapid – and erroneous – speculation. Was he studying the tactics of the enemy the better to counterattack, or was he moved by genuine interest in the rival faith? Neither; like a great part of the French population this week, he was anxious, possibly desperate, to have the latest news of the "Tour de France". The "Tour de France" has some claims to being the oddest sporting event in the world. It is a bicycle race round France, throwing in Belgium and Luxembourg for measure.

Day after day the *géants de la route* pedal along, preceded and followed by cars full of officials and reporters, and two or three times a day millions of the faithful listen to the radio or read notices in windows so as to have the latest news, while waiting for the detailed accounts and results in the papers.

At first sight a long-distance bicycle race would seem to be about the dullest possible form of competitive sport. But let those who think that the French are a frivolous people note their devotion to this tedious performance. It is a genuine devotion. Of course the fact that this is the first Tour de France since the war makes it of symbolic importance, a ground for hope that perhaps the good old days of 1939 are back again.

In their present alarming, if not desperate, situation it is natural that the French should cling to any evidence of what President Harding called "normalcy". But there is more in it than that. For what are (to me) unfathomable reasons lots of intelligent Frenchmen find some strange fascination in the Tour. "It is the only sporting event I ever read about in the papers," said an eminent and far from sedentary scholar.

That showed devotion indeed, for it is in the accounts of the Tour that the professional weakness of the sporting journalist reaches its height: the passion for jargon, for bogus idiom, for irrelevant moralising. "Yes, one of the star performers is doing it for the 'little woman'. So far 'the kiddies' are mercifully called in!"

Yet the reporters of the Tour deserve more sympathy than blame! Think of having to write thousands of words a day on such a monotonous theme as the tactics and results of a bicycle race! Was the Italian star really holding himself back in the sprint? How would the Swiss do when it came to the high mountain passes? Did so-and-so injure himself badly by his fall? But even speculation has its limits, so the unfortunate reporters are reduced to moral reflections on courage, etc., and to interesting little essays on the scenery. The landscape of Luxembourg is happily compared to a white jersey (the token of victory in each day's race is the *maillot jaune*), and at a time of multiple crisis in every department of French life, nearly two out of four pages of the popular papers are devoted to this stuff – and the Communists (who know their business) flank the photographs of Maurice Thorez with the latest news from the cycling front.

FISHERMAN WINS TOUR DE FRANCE

The Manchester Guardian, 21 July 1947

PARIS, JULY 20

Jean Robic, a Breton fisherman, today won the Tour de France, one of the world's greatest cycling races, after a ride of 26 days over 2,900 miles. Another Frenchman, Edouard Fachleitner, was second and Pierre Bramilla (Italy) third. Italy won the team prize.

SPORT AND COMMERCE IN THE TOUR DE FRANCE

by Philip Carr

The Manchester Guardian, 21 July 1949

The Tour de France is not only a great sporting event. It is an important commercial enterprise. It is important for the riders, who are nearly all working men and not yet professionals, though their expenses are paid by the organisers of the race. They hope to win some of the £10,000 which these organisers distribute in prizes and also some of the local prizes, of £50 and sometimes more, which towns on the route offer for the best time for their particular stage. They also expect to sign lucrative contracts for taking part, later in the summer, in velodrome competitions and exhibition rides all over the country.

The organisers have declared that their expenses this year will come to more than £70,000, of which £2,000 will be handed to the State for the privilege of closing the public roads. These expenses include not only the keep of the riders but a large and efficient first-aid service following them in motor-cars, and a mobile repair unit for their bicycles.

How are these expenses covered and a profit made? First there is the ransom paid by every town which is the terminus of one stage and the starting point of the next. These towns make considerable direct profit by lodging and feeding and garaging not only the competitors and the organisers but the whole army of newspaper men and their cars, as well as other cars which are allowed to follow the race – at a price. But, apart from this direct profit, there is the advertisement which a town wanting to become known as watering place will derive from being a halt in the Tour.

HUMANITÉ'S ENTERPRISE

It must not be supposed, however, that no limit is set to what a town chosen as a halt can do to win back some of the money it has paid. Last year the Communist paper *L'Humanité* ran an enormous motor-caravan which provided music for dancing at every halt – and political propaganda as well. So this year the Ministry of the Interior has stepped in and has forbidden the inclusion of any vehicle which advertises a newspaper or proclaims the views of a political party. This year, the experiment is being tried of making certain stages into time competitions, with the riders being started singly at fixed intervals, instead of all together. To each rider is attached an advertising lorry, drawn by lot, so that the whole race becomes an alternating procession of sport and advertisement. How marks are allotted in this contest I have never been able to understand; but probably every French village schoolboy could tell you.

EDITORIAL: TOUR DE FRANCE

The Manchester Guardian, 13 July 1950

Britain has its Cup Final; France has its Tour de France, which begins this morning. But if football's hour of glory casts reflections down the length of a day, cycling enjoys in the Tour de France a sort of apotheosis for every minute of the best part of month. So much so that it has become a Lord Mayor's show as well as a race. The managers and trainers who follow the cyclists as they pursue their 3,000-mile course round France and into Belgium, through towns and countryside and mountain ranges, are themselves followed by a motley procession of cars advertising such-and-such a commodity that So-and-so (one of the prima donnas of the race) is using on his machine. And then there are the hordes of enthusiasts who noisily line the route and throw bouquets at their favourites. (There never fails to be at least one incident of some zealous bouquet-thrower upsetting a rider and causing a minor uproar.) And last but not least there are the newspapers. The sports writers fill columns and columns during the race with tactics to a certain degree and figures and gossip to a greater one. The fascination of the race is obviously that it is so outstandingly the most statistical, the biggest, and best thing of its kind. Everything about it is worth close attention, from the weight of bananas the contestants eat to the quarrels that flare up between touchy stars. For there is plenty of competition about the whole affair, not merely on the personal but on the national level. Italians, Belgians, Dutch, Swiss, and others, as well as the French send their teams. The atmosphere is excited, tense; almost as tense, the French say, as the international situation. So, they feel, not logically perhaps but with eminent common sense, that it will help them to forget it. And if they are present at the start they can always see Orson Welles give their champions a send-off to-day. That should be relaxing.

ITALY'S CYCLISTS WITHDRAW: AN "ACE" UPSET

The Manchester Guardian, 27 July 1950

A large cloud has suddenly obscured Franco-Italian relations. Signor Bartali, the cyclist "ace" and the hero of most Italian youths, and the whole Italian cycling team suddenly withdrew last night from the Tour de France. All are returning to Italy today.

Something awful seems to have happened in the Pyrenees during the eleventh day of the race round France, just at the hardest climb when Bartali shot away to the head of the hundred pedallers from half a dozen nations. Here, according to most accounts (which share all the headlines with Korea), the Italian "ace" was deliberately thrown off his bicycle and beaten up by angry French youths, while according to all the papers here, "for four previous days Italian cyclists and journalists following the race had been greeted with cries of 'Salauds', 'Macaroni', hisses and even spits."

SLOW

Cycle races seem to be very tricky affairs and the mere amateur would be surprised to learn, for instance, from the *Stampa's* correspondent that "for days the French sporting press had most erroneously and arbitrarily accused the young Italian cyclists (the "cadets" as they are called) of barracking, of using brakes and slowing down the whole race, and of thus creating among the spectators an incredibly hostile attitude towards Italy".

The facts, as recounted by M. Goddet (the promoter of the whole Tour), are that a French press motor-cyclist with a photographer on the pillion barged in front of Bartali on the Col d' Aspin, in the Pyrenees, and caused him to fall. "These pressmen will not be allowed to follow the Tour any more," said Goddet.

Bartali's statement, made at midnight last night in Perpignan, does not mention the motor-cyclist. "After a continual rain of insults from the crowds, who kept closing in and allowed me no space to cycle, I was hit on the head," he says. "I did not fall at once, but veered and so brought Robic off his bicycle. We both fell. A fellow came and hit me. Another took my bicycle. I hit back and got my bicycle and rode on."

NOT SO SLOW

The descent from Col d'Aspin into Perpignan seems to have been achieved by Bartali at the record speed of 80 kilometres an hour. He came in first, shouting "I've been assaulted and I am going home." The last time a whole national team withdrew from the Tour de France was in 1937 when Belgium withdrew. On a previous occasion it appears that one Italian cyclist was beaten up and tied to tree. This sport is far from mild.

FRENCH APOLOGISE FOR CYCLE RACE INCIDENTS

The Manchester Guardian, 28 July 1950

The French Foreign Office has apologised to the Italian Embassy in Paris for the actions of some exuberant cycling enthusiasts in Southern France, and has promised that an inquiry would be held into Tuesday's series of incidents involving Italian riders in the Tour de France cycle race. The Italian national team withdrew from the race because of the incidents, during which the Italian rider Gino Bartali had to be protected from spectators.

TWO VIEWS ON A FAMOUS RACE

From a Special Correspondent
The Manchester Guardian, 25 July 1953

PARIS, JULY

After a brisk but unsuccessful effort to excite me about the Tour de France cycling race of 2,780 miles in 22 stages, which began at Strasbourg on July 3 and ends in Paris on Sunday, a French friend said, "Perhaps we could compare it with your Test cricket matches, about which there is so much in your newspapers, and which mystify us." "My friend," said I, "Test cricket and the Tour de France have nothing in common. For one thing …"

But there were 50 things. He had failed to impress me. I failed to impress him. I admitted that in some quarters in England the Test matches are unnecessarily dramatised. I tried to explain cricket's educational potentialities. My scoring rate improved, I thought, when I dealt with the history and literature of the game.

"Is there no advertising at the Test matches?" asked my friend. "Are not the crowds prayed, through loud-speakers, to buy this or that apéritif, lipstick, haircream or cheese?" I said that, although I had not seen a Test match this year, I would be surprised if the crowds were so beseeched. "Do the teams march round the ground behind a band?" "Certainly not." "Or enter the arena with glamour, like bullfighters?" "Oh no."

I back-pedalled slightly. "Those apéritifs. Three of – at any rate, one of them would make some cyclists ride in circles. Kindly explain the relationship however remote, between high-powered potations and sport." "It doesn't exist," said my Frenchman. "All this publicity, this ... er ... this ..."

"Americanisation?" I ventured.

"Not in the least. This ... er ... braying commercialisation was spontaneous. It began between the wars, with small cars advertising wares. This year, 80 publicity vehicles are on the road, using microphones through which the virtues of wares are proclaimed, while handbills are showered upon the multitude."

"Sounds costly," I said.

"All told about £1,600 for a lorry. The Tour de France, like most things in my country, gets costlier. The bill for this year's race will be about £150,000. Part of the money comes from municipalities of towns which the race puts on map. Some of the stages end during cycling meetings, the arrival of the Tour men being the star event. These meetings also bring money to the Tour, which along its entire route has about fifteen million spectators, who pay nothing. The winner gets, say, £6,000, counting his prize and contracts that fame brings. When I was young only cycle-makers used the Tour for propaganda. Nowadays even famous singers join in, giving open-air concerts to huge microphone-fed crowds where the riders stop."

My friend asked if I would like to see the publicity caravan when it arrived in Paris. "Next year, perhaps," I said. "There'll be a Tour next year?" "Almost certainly. This is the fiftieth anniversary of the race. We sadly need a French victory, for we have had only one since the war. And firms are saying that the … er … the" "Ballyhoo?" "That the ballyhoo costs too much. Won't you see the caravan?"

The whole caravan … Twelve teams, each of ten riders, started: a France team, five French regional teams, and teams from Belgium, Holland, Italy, Luxembourg, Spain, and Swit-zerland. Twelve thousand police and gendarmes are doing special duty for the Tour. In the caravan you would see 400 cars carrying officials, trainers, mechanics, masseurs, doctors, newspaper and radio reporters, and photographers.

"It takes a year to organise the race," continued my friend. "Always there are innovations. This year, owing to pressure from hotelkeepers, rooms in which the riders are treated with embrocation and other pungent concoctions will be scientifically deodorised for the benefit of holiday-making guests, to whom perhaps, the Tour de France means nothing."

He gave me a sharp look, sighed, and added: "I perceive that it means little to you. We will admit that my interest in your Test matches is small and call this a draw, with no score."

A BRITISH TEAM COMPETING

The Manchester Guardian, 7 July 1955

LE HAVRE, JULY 6

A British team is competing for the first time in the forty-second Tour de France cycle race which begins here to-morrow. There are 130 entrants. The course is about 4,458 kilometres (2,684 miles) long and runs from the Channel coast through the north of France, through Belgium and Luxembourg to the Vosges mountains of Alsace, into Switzerland, over the French Alps and up from Pau to Paris through the West and Centre of France.

France's chief hope is Louis Bobet, the world champion, who has won two consecutive tours. No-one has yet won a third time running. The Italian team will be without its leading cyclist, Fausto Coppi, and the greatest rival to Bobet is considered to be Stan Ockers of Belgium.

THE DISRUPTION OF A NATION

by St John Donn Byrne

The Observer, 10 July 1955

Last July, an American television producer came to Europe eager for new ideas and settled into a suite at one of those Paris hotels which are named after British royalty and patronised almost exclusively by the American rich. He then sent for a television set and sat down to milk the Gallic genius in his own particular field. Ten days later (so Art Buchwald says) he was asked what he thought of French television. He answered gloomily that every time he looked at the set there seemed to be some sort of bicycle race going on.

The producer had struck an unlucky moment for making sense of the normal French media of expression since the country was in its three-week annual disruption over the Tour de France. Radio, television, the Free Press, café gossip and the talk of the bar-proppers at this time are overwhelmingly focused on this feverish event which sticks to the edge of long and lonely roads through France – and this year through Belgium, Switzerland, and a 10-mile stretch of Germany.

WHOLE PAGES

Old-timers, though still in their twenties, will tell you that Tour de France is not what it was, that it has become commercialised beyond belief, and that the system of teams working for a particular man to win has limited the element of speculation. None the less, it holds its grip on the country, and whole pages of the press are given to it. It has the popularity of a Cup Final which lasts three weeks, and there is no need to go up for this particular cup since the whole thing may well be passing through your village.

There are 132 entries in this year's race and 10 of them are British. They are not regarded as serious challengers for the ultimate *maillot jaune*, which goes to the man who rides into Paris on July 30 with the highest placings for the Tour. The newspaper *Figaro* gives the British team a welcome, but says they are unfamiliar names which may make it difficult for the crowd to exhort them with such cries as "Vas-y Maitland!" and "Tue-les, Wood Revis!"

TOUR DE FRANCE NOTEBOOK

by John Gale
The Observer, 17 July 1955
MONTE CARLO

When you meet it the Tour de France bicycle race really strikes you as the only important thing in the world. It is hypnotic. It went through Briançon the other day in the kind of sunshine that taps the skull. Briantçon, in the Hautes-Alpes, is the highest town in Europe – a bald, slaty town of 7,000 most independent-minded citizens. The place was all *en fête*: the Tour was coming and it was *le Quatorze Juillet.*

The flags of the seven competing nations whispered on their high poles beside the palings lining the finish of the eighth stage of the race. It was dusty and crowded, and the air was loud with the recorded music of accordions. On all sides were mountains splashed with pine and snow.

Away outside the town, opposite the arrival point, sat the head of the Department of Agriculture of the Hautes-Alpes and his small son. "He's crazy, the boy," said the official. "Look! He's eating his pen. He's all worked up. Me, I don't like the Tour de France, you know."

"Bonjour à tous." The voice came from a huge tube of what looked like toothpaste, but was designed to make women's hair supple and shiny. It was motoring into the arrival area. "*Et voici les motos acrobates de Cinzano*": swarthy Martians standing on the saddles of ferocious, over-equipped motor-bikes.

The rolling flood of metal-voiced publicity continued to pass for more than an hour: the crews – one in a Free Forest's cap – tossing unimaginable sample products to the crowds. A banner proclaimed that a mineral water firm was sponsoring the eighth stage and awarding the £200 prize to the day's winner. "You see," said the agricultural official, "it is all far too commercial nowadays." He thought the sporting side was non-existent. "My department used to run a big trailer of free samples of perfumes and milk – 29 per cent fat content. But not any more. Oh no!"

On the Col du Galibier, well over 8,000ft, and with deep snow flanking the road, the riders were grimacing their way towards the top, some being given an illegal push (even begging, "*poussez*") or well-aimed buckets of water (legal).

At the summit there was a monument to Henri Desgranges, who started the Tour 52 years ago. The mountain, far from any village, was alive with spectators.

"Charley Gaul is now eight kilometres from the point of arrival."

"*Il n'est past loin, alors,*" said the crowd (a remark that goes on all day). At last he flashed by in a red shirt, fair hair, pedalling easily (a look of ease means style as in any sport). "*Comme il est jeunne!*"

Next, the *peloton*, and among them sprinting for the line, Louison Bobet, ("*Louison le magnifique*"), the world champion and winner of the Tour for the past two years, hero of France. The disapproving agriculturist was now on his feet like an unpractised man suddenly called upon to catch a cricket ball. "Louison, *poussez!*" Sweat on many spiky brown legs shone in the sun. A small dog ran on to the course and the Tour's travelling captain of *gendarmerie* blew his whistle and shouted "*Attrapez-le!*" and "*Vas-y Medor*" so long and so loudly that the dog became hysterical!

To accompany the Tour for the full three weeks and 22 stages (2,700 miles at 25mph) would be good way of getting to know the French: you would see over a third of the population. It is the biggest event ever.

Those who say it isn't sport have something, although the courage of the riders is unquestionable – the British team, on their first appearance, have done nobly. The Tour is, rather a sales campaign, brilliantly organised, and disorganising whatever part of France it touches (it has also slipped this year into Belgium, Luxembourg, Germany, and Switzerland).

It is said that this time the Tour is costing the organisers *L'Équipe* and *Le Parisien Libéré* £170,000: but it is doubtful whether it costs them anything like that in the end. Some wishing to advertise in the caravan must pay a set fee: £800, for instance, for a one-ton truck over the whole route, £80 for one day. Local chambers of commerce put up considerable sums to have their towns overrun (Briançon does not, since the Tour can scarcely avoid going through it even if it wanted to. But one of the Tour's chief organisers, who is a bit like a thin Jack Solomons, held frequent meetings with the town's hotel owners.) It is almost impossible to get into hotels when the Tour is near, and you may well spend the night on some remote mountain in the back of a small car that is not designed for sleep.

Riders are under rigorous contract. Everything is provided for them – shirts and shorts are washed every night. Most get a flat rate of about £4 day. There are prizes of £200 for winning a stage and several other awards laid on by factories and commercial firms on the route.

The winner of the whole Tour (he need not even win a stage, but must have the highest average placing when he reaches Paris on July 30) usually gets about £4,000, half of which he usually gives to his team. But the victory will bring him big contracts and advertising fees (they say that Coppi, the greatest road-racing champion ever, once made £70,000 in year). Likely winners of the Tour will try not to allow serious rivals to break away and win a stage, but they are not worried if stages are won by "*outsidaires*" with no overall placing, from whom they have nothing to fear.

It seems that a rider may quite often be allowed – provided he is no threat – to win in the part of France from which he comes: this will bring him big local contracts the following year. Most of the members of a team are *domestiques* – servants

– whose job is to serve the team's star and its two other best riders. They do this by sacrificing their own chances; by acting as windbreaks and by helping a star in any way they can if he breaks down.

There is also a team car, carrying the team's manager, a mechanic and a *commissaire*, or umpire, and spares to help with repairs and to dictate tactics – such as sending a *domestique* back several kilometres to help another rider.

Those who knew racing in the past say that these tactics have also affected the sport: the stages were once as long as 400 kilometres, and it was every man for himself (slow riders would arrive just in time for the next day's stage). A famous rider was once winning the Tour by as much as an hour when his front forks broke: he dashed into a blacksmith's and remade the forks himself, while the blacksmith – forbidden to help by regulations – looked on. This man eventually came second, and a plaque has since been erected in his honour.

The Tour reached the garish haven of Monte Carlo last night, a stage of 275 kilometres. It crossed four passes (one just under 10,000ft) and flew down many slippery hairpin bends at nearly 60mph – in lightning, hail, cloudburst, and then oppressive heat.

Of the 130 riders who started, about two-thirds are left in the Tour. This is a rare week-end of rest. Robust young men in track suits are sitting, covered with huge patches of sticking-plaster, under gleaming chandeliers in the *fin de siècle* hotels. To-day the British team had roast beef for lunch in the Hotel Beau Séjour.

DON'T PUSH

The Manchester Guardian, 30 July 1955

A list of fines on competitors issued by judges of the Tour de France cycling race, which ends today, gives the names of fifteen riders who have to pay 30 shillings each for receiving their third "unsolicited push". Five others are fined £2 each for getting a fourth unrequested shove. No one figures in the list as an actual applicant for a push. Fines in such cases are presumably heavier. A rider fined for receiving an unsolicited shove vowed he had made no request. Evidence said he had winked at a spectator in a manner which could be interpreted only as a supplication for propulsion. Every year newspapers, the radio, and loudspeakers on the route implore Tour de France spectators to abstain from pushing the riders even if, as may happen during the hill-climbing, they appear to be at the end of their resources. Unknown to the judges some potent winking may have been going on.

BOBET WINS AGAIN: ENGLISHMAN'S PLUCK IN TOUR DE FRANCE

The Manchester Guardian, 1 August 1955

Louison Bobet, the French cyclist, gained the first "hat-trick" in the Tour de France by winning for the third year running. His time when he rode into the Parc des Princes Stadium at the end of the 2,775 miles was 130hr 29min 26sec.

There was special cheer for Tony Hoar, a plumber from Emsworth, Hampshire, whose determination to finish the course had earned him the admiration of the French. He was an amateur until six months ago. As he passed walls and bridges along the route – usually last – he was greeted with chalked slogans of "Vive Hoar".

Hoar and Brian Robinson, who was twenty-ninth with an aggregate time of 132hr 26min 36sec, were the only two British riders left out of the team of ten. Altogether, 69 riders completed the course out of 110 starters. Hoar was bottom of the list, though he and Robinson were placed equally ninth on the last lap from Tours to Paris. Both agreed that they had been up against the world finest hill-climbers in the French cyclists, who won the team championship.

GREAT WIN FOR ANQUETIL

The Manchester Guardian, 22 July 1957

J. Anquetil (France) won the 2,900-mile Tour de France, the most arduous cycle race in the world, which ended in Paris on Saturday. Anquetil, who is 23 years old, led for 15 of the 22 stages in the race, which began on June 27. Only 56 of the original 120 starters set out on the last stage. Anquetil's time was 135hr 44min 42sec.

Anquetil who is outstanding as a time trialist and middle-distance rider, proved himself great all-rounder. He consolidated his lead by winning the 66-kilometre (41-mile) time trial at the twentieth stage. After that, only an accident could have robbed him of victory. M. Janssens (Belgium) was second with 135hr 59min 38sec, and A. Christian (Switzerland) third, with 136hr 2min 2sec. With only the two rest days, the riders have been whipped by winds and rain, scorched by the sun, and some bruised by spills as they toiled along a route which took them over several mountains, sometimes over 7,000 feet. Winner of the last stage of 227 kilometres (141 miles) from Tours to Paris was A. Darrigade (France), who took 5hr 58min 31sec.

R. Harris (Britain), former world sprint cycling champion, finished third in the Grand Prix held in conjunction with the finish of the Tour de France. He led in the final, but got shut in on the last bend and finished third to R. Gaignard, the French champion, and A. Maspes, Italian holder of the world title.

FRIDAY ON A BICYCLE

by Pendennis
The Observer, 13 July 1958

The fact that a Yorkshireman, Brian Robinson (a name up to now known in Paris only as a Metro Station), has been bicycling magnificently in the three-week Tour de France, and has already won one lap, has aroused Frenchmen. The sporting *L'Équipe* sees Robinson as Man Friday, "the savage who learns the gestures of our civilisation", and who will in turn teach civilised cycling to his fellow savages.

The *Canard* takes a similar line "We shall see the repercussions of Robinson's win throughout *la vielle Angleterre* – a fine revenge for the crushing defeat in the World Cup. The 'little Queen' will abandon racing. We are already reliably informed that Prince Philip cycles diligently to Buckingham, and that Churchill himself will become an expert."

"TOLEDO EAGLE" WINS THE TOUR

The Observer, 19 July 1959

Federico Bahamontes, a 31-year-old Spaniard, won the Tour de France which ended here today. Britain's representatives, Brian Robinson (Huddersfield) and Vic Sutton (Sheffield), finished nineteenth and thirty-seventh. Bahamontes, nicknamed the "Toledo Eagle" because of his climbing powers in the mountain stages, is the first Spaniard to win the Tour. Belgium won the team event. The last stage of the 22-stage 2,706-mile race, which started on June 25, was won by Joseph Groussard, of France.

CHAPTER THREE
MODERN GLORY

Tour de France by J. B. Wadley

Anquetil's a cert

Route of the Tour de France—2,500 miles and three weeks of punishing pedalling.

BRITISH journalists, in trying to convey something of the atmosphere of the Tour de France, have long employed the device of saying that the excitement is like the Cup Final, a Test match and the Derby rolled into one.

This year one must settle for Wembley and Lord's, for there is something missing.

True, the 48th Tour is bigger than ever. It is costing more—£300,000—to put on. Prize money is higher; £50,000 must be won. Radio and television coverage by a score of Continental stations is wider, and the British housewife who can't switch on without getting "that wretched Test" has her French counterpart who is haunted for three weeks by "*Ce maudit Tour.*"

The missing something is the usual uncertainty. Can a Frenchman win? This year everybody is certain he will. It is not that Jacques Anquetil born and bred in Rouen is so far above his principal rivals that the men who might have given him a race will not be there.

Last year's winner, Nencini, had an accident early in the season, got back somewhere near form only to crash again in the recent Tour of Switzerland and scratch from the Tour de France.

Neither is Pambianco in the Italian team. He beat Anquetil in the Tour of Italy, and is now being treated like the great Coppi himself by an admiring public. It is said that his Italian sponsors do not wish to see him knocked off that pedestal by Anquetil in the return contest.

It is probable that Anquetil will take over race leadership tomorrow afternoon and keep the *maillot jaune* throughout the 21 stages. Only one man has done this, Romain Maes, of Belgium, in 1935.

Anquetil is solidly backed by 11 Frenchmen who have his written guarantee that he will share all his prize money with them

By carrying his bat throughout the 2,500-mile innings Anquetil might boost the team kitty up to the £20,000 mark.

On paper his only danger is from Charly Gaul, of Luxembourg, the star climber who is known as the Angel of the Mountains.

When the teams were introduced at the local Cirque last night three of Britain's principal men were missing; Brian Robinson, Shay Elliott and Tom Simpson. The first two were delayed after racing in Belgium, but there was general concern over the non-appearance of Simpson.

"How is Tom's knee?" a dozen journalists asked me. Later I found Simpson at his hotel just in after seeing a specialist in Paris.

"It should be all right as long as I take it steady," he explained.

CYCLISTS PAY TRIBUTE

by Norris McWhirter

The Observer, 10 January 1960

Europe's most emotional funeral of a sport star since the streets of Paris were lined for Suzanne Lengleo, in 1938, took place at Castellania, in Southern Italy, on Monday. Fausto Coppi, twice winner of the Tour de France (1949 and 1952), was buried in the graveyard of the old, white-walled church. Thousands of cyclists and a high proportion of women converged on the funeral service. Other famous riders, such as Bobet, Darrigade and Bartali, threw flowers on Coppi's coffin. Police had considerable difficulty in preventing the vast throng from penetrating beyond the cemetery walls. The cause of Coppi's death on January 2 was a malarial virus and typhus which he picked up on a trip to Africa. Raphael Geminiani, the famous French cyclist who was his companion on the trip, also fell seriously ill but is now considered to be out of danger.

"THE SPARROW" SOARS

by Norris McWhirter

The Observer, 10 April 1960

Continentals are really becoming excited about the deeds of one of the two Britons ever to exhibit the qualities necessary for victory in their gruelling 2,700-mile Tour de France.

He is "The Sparrow", otherwise known as Tom Simpson, 22, of Doncaster, who is beginning to overshadow even Brian Robinson. On April 3 he trounced an all-star field in the Mont Faron hill-climb over 16.46 miles in 46min 44sec, beating the Spaniard Gil, the German record-breaker Rudi Altig, and the 1948 Tour winner Charley Gaul of Luxembourg.

When Simpson chose the 1959 world road championship for his professional début he had the temerity to hold the lead for 120 miles. He now has to make up his mind on the priorities of attacking the world record or riding for greater rewards in next summer's Tour.

A MAN TO SHOCK THE FRENCH

by Christopher Brasher
The Observer, 26 June 1960

A thin man with close-cropped dark hair and a beak of a nose uncoils himself from a chair in a Paris shop and comes to meet you. He is wearing a well-pressed Prince of Wales check suit, white shirt, silk tie and black Italian-style shoes. He looks like a very comfortably off, well-paid Parisian. In fact he is one of the greatest English athletes of 1960 – and one of the least known.

His name is Tommy Simpson, he is 22 years old and he has been a professional cyclist for nine months – the most successful first nine months that any professional cyclist, whatever his nationality, has ever had.

Today he starts from Lille to circle France on his bicycle, riding some 2,600 miles in 21 stages as a member of the second British team ever to compete in the Tour de France. He will tell you that neither he nor the team has any chance of winning. He means it. And he is right.

But one July day in this decade Tommy Simpson seems very likely to ride through Paris and into the Parc des Princes wearing the yellow jersey of the overall Tour leader; and the French will be as shocked as we would be if they were to win a Test series in this country. But when he does, he will probably still be almost unknown in this insular island.

Simpson is a fine example of a new class of young Englishman of this decade to whom frontiers, strange currencies and languages mean little. He is uninhibited and determined, and he may soon shock the Continental cycling world as much as Herb Elliott shocked the international athletic world in 1958.

First bronze

Yet Simpson does not come from any pioneer country but from County Durham. He was born on November 30, 1937, which makes him seem so much younger than his achievements. At 16 he won the national junior hill climb championship and came third in the senior. At 18 he was competing in the Olympic Games in Melbourne, winning a bronze medal in the 4,000 metres team pursuit and at 20 he seemed to have a chance for the world championship, but in a heat his wheel hit a groove and he fell and fractured his jaw.

When he had recovered he threw up his job as an engineering draughtsman and took himself and his savings to Zurich to attack, unsuccessfully, the world hour record. He started in 1959 as an amateur and did very well but was surprised to find that some of those Continentals whom he had thought inferior to himself in the world amateur championships the year before were doing very well as professionals.

He thought the time had come for him to break into the Continental circus, so he wrote to the British Cycling Federation for permission to compete abroad as an independent (a half-way stage between amateur and professional) and set off for France on April 1 1959, with £100 in his pocket.

If he had not made something of a name by the time his money ran out he would return home. He went to Brittany, mainly because he knew two young French cyclists whose family lived in St Brieuc and who had offered to put him up, but also because it was new territory for an English cyclist – most of those who had gone to the Continent started in Belgium. He needed no more than £15 of that hundred. He won a *prime* (a small prize for leading at an intermediate stage) in his first race and won the second outright.

LONELY AND CUT OFF

Despite these quick successes he felt very lonely and cut off. He didn't know the language and had few friends. Many times he thought that he was a fool to be trying to break into one of the toughest and most professional sports in the world. When he sent home newspaper cuttings of his first successes, English riders did not believe they were true. Every French rider was considered to be a Rivière or an Anquetil, and it was inconceivable that a young Englishman should be beating them.

Simpson says that British athletes are the best in the world. "Their standard of living and their upbringing is better than almost any other European country and, besides, Britain is the best country in the world. But we just have no confidence in ourselves. We make our opponents bigger than they actually are. Really, you know, Britain isn't a sporting nation. We laugh a bit at the French in sport but it is they who go and watch any sport."

Gradually Simpson's confidence began to improve and he rose from being a good local rider to a good national rider. The manager of one of the big teams – sponsored by St Raphael the *apéritif* firm – asked him if he would sign on for two years. Simpson had arrived. He turned professional and now he had an assured weekly income whether he was riding or not.

When the season ended in November he came back to England and took a holiday. He needed it and from the end of November to the middle of January he only got on to a bike twice.

In January this year he went to the South of France, where most of the French teams were doing their early season training, and there he began to build up his strength and stamina again. When the season started Simpson immediately jumped into the front rank of riders and found it hard to control his patience when he was held back by the team manager to protect the team's stars Geminiani and Rivière. New boys to a team have to act as "domestics", or servants, to the stars.

Several times he was within a few kilometres of winning a classic race only to be caught at the finish. The French press started by saying he was unlucky. When the same thing happened again and again they said he was unintelligent.

Simpson is certainly not that. It is simply that he is not content to become a first-class rider – he wants to be the best in the world. Not for him the win by a wheel length in a tight sprint at the end of a 125-mile race. He goes out to break the opposition early on and if he has to do it alone, he will. If the field catches him before the finishing line then that is because he has not yet got enough strength. But give him a year or two more to develop and they will not catch him.

Already the man many experts consider most likely to win today's first or tomorrow's second stage of the Tour is – Tommy Simpson. "Of course I won't be able to keep it up. We just haven't got a big enough or strong enough team, but a first stage win would give me a lot of confidence and put up my starting price for events after the Tour."

Strangely enough, for all the vast amount of money that is poured into the Tour – about £175,000 – a rider does not expect to get much of it. The overall winner distributes all his prize money among his team, for without them he could never have won. Nevertheless a Tour winner can expect to make £20,000–£140,000 in a year from starting money and advertising. Bahamontes of Spain, who won the 1959 Tour, is a very rich man.

Simpson owes a lot to Brian Robinson, the Huddersfield rider who has ridden the Continental circuit for five or six years now and who has won two stages in past Tours. Robinson, at 29, will never be great rider but he is a thoroughly competent *domestique* and *domestiques* can earn a very reasonable living. Robinson has just built himself a £5,000 house in Yorkshire and has a share in a building company. He and Simpson also share a flat in Paris.

Landy, in 1954, proved that Australian athletes could make their mark in Europe; Elliott, in 1958, proved that they could also produce a class of athlete who was unbeatably superior to the rest of the world. If Robinson has done for British cycling what Landy did for Australian athletics, Simpson may well be the Elliott of the cycling world.

FROM BOOS TO CHEERS

by JB Wadley

The Observer, 16 July 1961

TOURS, JULY 15

André Darrigade of the French National team to-day won the 192-mile twentieth stage of the Tour de France from Périgueux to here. But Jacques Anquetil, with his splendid win yesterday in the 46 and a half mile time trial between Bergerac and Périgueux increased his lead over Charly Gaul to 10 minutes, and made certain of overall victory.

Yesterday the July 14 holiday crowds cheered him. Tomorrow, when he rides his lap of honour at the Parc des Princes track in Paris, he will not expect so unanimous a vote of approval, even though he will have carried out his promise and worn the *maillot jaune* from the first to the last day. The public likes a race, and there hasn't been one in the Tour this year. The fault is not Anquetil's but his rivals'. If Anquetil has any weakness, it is in the mountains. Yet never in the two Pyrenean stages during the week was he in danger. Indeed the much heralded four-col stage, which included the climb of the 7,000-ft Tourmalet, was a complete flop.

LACK OF FIGHT

Charly Gaul, the challenger, and Anquetil and other leaders on general classification climbed together in a tight little pack while a regional rider, Queheille, broke away and dropped them by nearly three minutes. If a section of the crowd does boo Anquetil tomorrow, it will be because they are unable to dissociate him from the French national team which he captains. Besides slowing down the race, the "chase everybody" policy of the Tricolors has robbed many a lesser light of the chance of getting in the headlines and the money. If it had been left to Anquetil's challengers, the Tour would have been a leisurely ride. To the rescue last week came a number of humbler riders, among them our three survivors, Elliott, Laidlaw and Robinson, who nearly brought off a hat-trick of wins in the daily "most aggressive rider" category.

First Elliott earned the title (and £80), then Laidlaw (£95), and Robinson seemed well on the way to top marks when he surprisingly faltered on the Tourmalet climb. Laidlaw is the surprise of the race. During he week he had the satisfaction of getting away from Gaul on the mountain climb and finishing eleventh in a massed sprint on the steeply banked track at Bordeaux. He had every reason to be pleased with his first Tour de France, but Robinson and Elliott are both disappointed men.

BIG BUSINESS IS BACK

by JB Wadley
The Observer, 8 October 1961

"The sporting sensation of the half-century" was how one Paris daily announced the midweek proposal to change the formula of the Tour de France. Instead of the 2,500-mile race being contested by national and French regional teams, the organisers are almost certain to revert to the trade team system. It wasn't really a sensation. Those who followed last year's dull affair knew something would have to be done to liven it up, and *marques* seemed the only remedy. The re-entry of the trade will certainly give the 1962 Tour a fillip, but whether the cure will be permanent remains to be seen. Some specialists think it will not. They remember the big business intrigues that threatened the Tour in the late 20s, and precipitated the abandonment of the trade team formula.

It is more than likely that pressure from wealthy Italian sponsors finally broke down the organisers' opposition to trade teams. The 1960 Tour was a poor one because world champion Rik Van Looy was not riding – persuaded to abstain by his Milan employers, it is said. Another dull year and the Tour de France would have been out of business.

The organisers – *L'Équipe* and *Parisien Libéré* – plan to break the new sequence of trade team races with a national team Tour every five years starting in 1965.

The proposal for 1962 is that 15 teams of nine riders will start the Tour from Nancy on June 24 and at least six men of each team must be of the same nationality. From the British point of view the new formula is welcome. Not that any British manufacturer is likely to be in the line-up – although the French cannot understand why – but on past form four riders are good enough to get places in French teams: Brian Robinson and Tom Simpson (Gitane Cycles), Shay Elliott and Alan Ramsbottom (Helyett Cycles). Britain will not, as this year, have to field a further eight riders unready for the hurly-burly of the Tour.

CYCLE TOUR MYSTERY

by JB Wadley
The Observer, 8 July 1962

CARCASSONE, FRANCE

Nine competitors retired from the Tour de France cycling marathon today, and their withdrawals have led to whispers that pep drugs have been taking their toll. At this stage it is impossible to be dogmatic about the cause of this mass fall-out, and one must rely on the official communiqué issued tonight by the event medical officer. This dismisses a claim that food poisoning was alone responsible for the retirements.

It says that "certain forms of preparation" – it does not specifically mention the word "dope" – might be the cause. In future, the communiqué concludes, the doctor will resume his visits to riders' hotels each night.

DRUG PEDALLING

by Peter Lennon

The Guardian, 22 July 1964

When the Tour de France riders came panting into the Parc des Princes, Paris, after a 2,800-mile jog around the nation, their muscles threadbare – some in a state of collapse – many of them must have realised that they were probably the last representatives of old-style, heart-tearing cycle racing. A few days before, the Secretary of State for Sport, M. Maurice Herzog, had announced that this autumn the French Assembly will vote on, and without any doubt pass, a law forbidding the use of stimulants in sport.

This new law will be enforced by a team of 700 State-employed doctors throughout the country and the heavy penalties, fines, imprisonment, and disqualification which go with it are aimed not only at any sportsman, native or foreign, performing in France but also at their trainers, managers and masseurs. With modern methods of detection it will no longer be necessary to perform a cumbersome analysis of sweat and saliva; a urine test on the spot will be sufficient to reveal the quantity and the kind of drugs that have been used.

Particularly in recent years, drug-taking has become so widespread in France – and in Italy and Germany – that in sports requiring long and intense effort excessive use of stimulants, such as benzedrine and weckamine, has become almost obligatory.

There is a strong probability that the standard of performance in cycling has been artificially raised by wholesale use of drugs, sometimes of a particularly dangerous variety. The Medical Officer of the Secretariat of State for Sport, Dr Perrier, told me that for some years now medical men whose work brings them in contact with sportsmen have been urgently demanding that something should be done about the use of drugs. Also the practice of taking vitamins in doses 15 or more times beyond the normal therapeutic quantity has spread to teenage amateur sportsmen. The example of their professional elders is largely responsible. And behind that are the vast commercial interests which bully and bribe their sportsmen to greater efforts.

Unlike vitamins, such as glucose, which aid in conserving the suppleness of the muscles and allow more prolonged effort, the drugs in common use act on the brain and the nervous system, and give the sportsman a false idea of his own powers, pushing him to perform feats which are in fact beyond his natural endurance. The use of artificial stimulants in sport can be traced back to antiquity and is generally found among primitive tribes – piote is one of the most common natural drugs.

Their use in modern times is generally linked with the experiments in heart-beat rhythms of Professor Gerschler, who many years ago was responsible for some of the tremendous performances by the celebrated runner Rudolf Harbig. Commercial interests cashed in on the possibilities and the production of drugs for sport has become a valuable industry – particularly in Germany.

One of the turning points in the French government's concern with this problem came four years ago when, at the end of the Tour des Flandres, 1960, a young cyclist, Jean Gracyzk, announced that in an agreement with his manager and with a journalist on the Paris sports daily *L'Équipe*, he had not used any drugs that season and had proved by his performance that he could do as well without them.

With this admission that drug taking had been a normal part of his training came a number of other revelations. A French journalist admitted that one of the great hopes of the Italians, Eugène Tamburlini, had told him that the previous year he had accepted a drug before the Grand Prix of the Nations and had been struck temporarily blind on the spot. A short time later he committed suicide in Rome.

Stories of cyclists finishing a particularly gruelling lap frothing at the mouth and wild accounts of German cyclists pausing on a country road to give themselves a needle were largely confirmed. Well-known cyclists admitted that they had no choice but to use "modern methods" if they hoped to stay on top. One of the men most active in the campaign against the use of drugs is Dr Dumas, the official medical officer of the Tour de France. He found that sports managers, while agreeing in principle that it would be desirable to eliminate drugs, feared that French sportsmen would be put at a disadvantage in competition with the German, Italian and Japanese opponents. But strict control of the Tour de France next year will put all competitors on a level. Already this year the first five home in the test of young talent, the Tour de l'Avenir, had to submit to urine tests, although there was as yet no law by which they could be condemned. France is one of the first countries in the world to tackle this problem seriously. Belgium is likely also to bring in a law very soon and Italy and Spain are expected to follow.

WATCHING FOR DOPE

by Andrew Mulligan

The Observer, 20 June 1965

While the public's attention will be focused on cycling, doctors will be on the look-out for signs of doping among the competitors such as was high-lighted in the Tour of Britain a week ago. Last December, the French Parliament passed an anti-doping law in which "it resolved to vigorously stamp out such degrading practices". In the debate that followed, there was unanimous agreement that "an athlete who is doped is a cheat for trying to artificially improve his performance". The French aim to be the first nation to have passed an anti-doping law. But there is the difficulty of defining the difference between what the French call "reconstituents" (stimulants) and physical dope.

Jean Bobet, brother of Louison Bobet, Sports Editor of Radio Luxembourg and former cycle champion, told me: "Doping is commonest in cycling because the races are principally endurance tests." Bobet went on to say that a great champion like his brother or Anquetil regularly took "reconstituents" but never took dope. "A doped cyclist could last only couple of seasons."

GODDET, THE MAN WHO MAKES THE WHEELS TURN

by Andrew Mulligan

The Observer, 4 July 1965

"The Tour de France," said Antoine Blondin, "is a mobile village – an anarchy with its own laws and customs, a territory 30 kilometres long and as wide as the road, ruled by a mayor who is Jacques Goddet. The laws of France cease to operate. The gendarmes are there not to enforce the laws of the State but the laws of the Tour. Goddet can perform marriages like a sea captain, no one, not even de Gaulle would dare raise his voice in anger if Goddet shot down a Russian or American who had violated his air space." He said it in jest before a leg of the Tour and after following it for a day I believe him.

Jacques Goddet, executive director of *L'Équipe*, who aspires to be Mayor of St Tropez, stood in his long British colonial shorts with a toupee on his Alec Guinness head, administrating the start of the night stage of the Tour with the calm of a district commissioner receiving a tribal delegation. Journalists gazed at him through mouthfuls of sea food and Muscadet, admiring the man who had conceived and modernised the Tour, which an American journalist once described as the best piece of organisation since the North African landings.

ON TO BORDEAUX

At the off that strange, whirring noise of 130 cyclists began to eat up the road to Bordeaux. Behind them, team cars covered with advertisements and spare bikes with their wheels spinning against a background of yacht masts in La Rochelle harbour, and to the left of them a stampeding horde of journalists and photographers. Goddet's co-director leads the riders while he sits just behind, calling up the team cars to change a puncture – done at Le Mans speed – or hauling a red flag up his aerial to stop following cars from passing the massed cyclists when the road is too dangerous or too narrow. It was always dangerous and mostly narrow. If there was no room to pass on the road the cars mounted the pavements and gave the spectators a thrill by sandwiching them on the kerb.

Italian car horns blared through the peaceful French countryside and one was glad that the Protestant facade of La Rochelle had been rid of the all-conquering Latin vulgarity of the Tour.

The road runs arrow-like over the undulating East Anglia-esque flat lands by the Atlantic, before it turns inland through the Romanesque vineyards of the Gironde and on down to Bordeaux.

Peasants' picnic

All France seemed to be picnicking: peasants hacked at bread and cheese or brought out antiquated telescopes, soldiers had the day off and provincial bourgeoisie sat at their respectable tables, forks in their hands and transistors in their ear. For a following journalist perhaps the greatest elation of all is the puerile feeling, known best to Heads of State, of riding a convertible, standing up on the seat, at full speed through the villages and acknowledging the clapping and cheering of women and children. One felt rather like General MacArthur on his recall from Korea.

If you looked behind at the straining hordes and incredible pace of cyclists you were soon deflated by their superlative physical condition. The brown, wind-polished limbs, traced with the suggestion of varicose veins, and the teamwork of getting a competitor back into the crowd as three or four team-mates slipstreamed the stricken rider from in front and the team car virtually pushed him from behind. The stage to Bordeaux is normally boring, except that it is the last before the mountains and often won by a Dutchman. The Pyrenees, which lie ahead, will sort out the real competitors before they reach Barcelona on Saturday evening.

DUTCH VICTORIES

Nobody quite knows why the Dutch win at Bordeaux, perhaps the final effort of the "flatlanders" before the Pyrenees or the celebration of arrival on familiar terrain after the Pyrenees – whichever way the Tour is run.

Some competitors feel that Poulidor, the French favourite, who has now moved to second place, has already won. Of the three Italians, young Felice Gimondi is in the lead, with Adorni and Motta all well placed. Poulidor himself said, "The mountains are our chance and we're going to seize it." The Spaniards think otherwise. "The Pyrenees", said the great climber Bahamontes", will be an entirely Spanish recital."

TOUR DE FRANCE '67

by Geoffrey Nicholson
The Observer, 25 June 1967

The Tour de France is more than the biggest cycle race of the year. After the Olympics and the World Cup, it is the most elaborate sports promotion in the world. It costs some £500,000 to stage, and it may be worth £15,000 to the winner; lasts 24 days and covers nearly 3,000 miles; is followed by 250 reporters and watched daily on television by 150 million European viewers. A race of fearful stress for its

130 riders, it is at the same time a gaudy travelling circus to advertise beer, chocolate, petrol, and bananas ("the fruit in the jersey").

TIME

The Tour is, in effect, a series of 22 one-day races of around 135 miles. Each of these stages is a separate event with its own prizes and prestige. But the race winner is the man who covers the total distance in the shortest time – which he can do without ever winning a stage. Within the race, too, there are various other kinds of contest. Next in value to wearing the race leader's yellow jersey is to win the green. This goes to the rider – usually someone with a prodigious sprint – who collects the best places at the stage finishes, regardless of time. This is a points competition; one point for first, two for second, and so on, with the lowest total taking the prize. Third most rewarding is the Grand Prix de la Montagne, for the man who picks up most *prime* points by climbing ahead of the rest over the passes of the Vosges, Alps, Pyrenees and the Massif Central.

There are also three time trials this year, two individual and one for teams. These have a staggered start, the riders competing not against each other but against the hands of the stop-watch. They favour the disciplined, self-sufficient men.

But the characteristic event of the Tour is the mass-start race over roads which, for several hours before, have been closed to all but emergency traffic. An hour or so ahead of the riders goes the publicity caravan. With them travel the police outriders, the matching Peugeots of the officials and team managers, and 60 press cars. Since the reporters can't all watch the race at the same time, most drive in front tuned in to the private commentaries from Radio Tour.

GLOSSARY

bidon, water bottle

col, mountain pass

contre la montre, time trial in which the riders set off individually at one-minute intervals to cover a short course unpaced against the stopwatch. In a team time trial each team is sent away separately and takes the time of the third man across the finishing line.

coureur, racing cyclist, often used as term of approval to distinguish a dedicated rider.

domestique, rider who is in the team not to win prizes for himself but to serve and protect his leader, also *porteur d'eau*.

Routier-sprinter, road-race cyclist noted for his finishing sprint.

grimpeur, a man recognised for his strength in the mountain stages, most famous since the war was the Spaniard, Federico Bahamontes "the Eagle of the Mountains".

lanterne rouge, last man overall at the end of the Tour.

maillot jaune, yellow jersey worn by the race leader.

maillot vert, green jersey worn by the leader on points classification.

musette, light satchel in which food is handed up to the riders as they pass the feeding points; they transfer the food to the pouch pockets of their racing jerseys and discard the bag.

peloton, main bunch of riders.

prime, intermediate prize for the first rider to reach a certain point along the route, especially the top of a mountain climb.

Roi des Montagnes, rider who wins most points in the mountain *primes*.

TACTICS

Tactics are a matter of attack and pursuit. At times there seems to be no contest. The whole field rides along at a club-run pace, almost in the doldrums. But then the attack will come. It may be a sustained spell of pressure by the important riders at the front, a trial of strength which winnows away the riders behind. Or it may be an escape. In ones or twos, or perhaps in a group of a dozen, riders will break away from the front and get clean away. The tactical problem then is whether or not to try to pursue them. The break may burn itself out. Or it may be composed of minor characters who are irrelevant to the overall struggle. But those who ignore an attack can never be quite certain that they haven't underrated its importance.

It's here that the leader depends on his team. If he gets away in a break, he expects his team to cluster at the front of the bunch, slowing its pace and hindering any pursuers. If it's a rival who escapes, he relies on his team to give chase. But, in the end, and especially in the mountains, only he can help himself. No Tour is ever won solely by a good team, any more than it's won without one.

There is far more tactics than strategy. Jacques Anquetil could calculate in advance how much time he could risk losing in the mountains, and then pull back in the time trials where he was almost unbeatable.

There is roughly £35,000 in prizes. It is worth £150 to win a stage, £75 a day to wear the yellow jersey early in the race, £37 later on when it tends to settle on the same person's shoulders. The green jersey man gets around £700, and the King of the Mountains £375 – plus his various *prime* prizes – from Chocolat Poulain.

Arthralgon laboratory products give up to £150 daily to the most aggressive rider, and Coper jams £37 to the most unfortunate, with £150 to the man who's suffered most over the three weeks. Outspan Oranges used to reward the rider who showed "the greatest amiability or the most agreeable nature". That seems to have disappeared from the prize lists, but a worthy successor has been found: Bachelier-Sports establishments offer £75 to the competitor who reveals the greatest elegance of clothing and comportment.

PUBLICITY

Nothing moves on the Tour without a salute to the sponsor. Singer washing machines do the riders' laundry. Arthralgon provide the ambulance and medical services. UNA supply the food the riders carry in their pouches (an average day's menu: ham and jam sandwiches, rice cakes, tarts, banana, pear, prunes, lumps of sugar, with two more bags of rations to be handed up during the journey).

The publicity caravan rolls ahead, whiling away time for the spectators: the Banana Committee with an accordionist who has sold a million discs, the Poulain clown who carries his weight in chocolate, the Chapigneuelles beer accordionist, the Esso tiger-striped cars, UNA's two young accordionists.

And in the stage town that evening Dalida will sing, the Haricot Rouges combo will play, and the Majorettes whirl their batons. There will be an open-air film of the day's stage, fireworks, dancing and more accordionists. And the riders, in their hotel bedrooms above the street, wonder when the whole thing will ever stop.

SIMPSON ALONE GIVES BRITAIN PRESENCE IN TOUR DE FRANCE

by Geoffrey Nicholson
The Guardian, 28 June 1967

Tomorrow evening in Angers, ten British cyclists will tighten their toe-straps, hump their shoulders and set out on the Tour de France. In fact their first journey will take them only three and a half miles in a brief, individual time trial. It will not offer much taste of the rigours to come in the next three weeks – the cobbles of the Nord, the slow, laborious drags across the Alps and Pyrenees, the interminable 215-mile stage back up through the centre of France on the next-to-last day.

If five of the ten reach the finish in Paris on July 23, it will be a minor national triumph. Yet it is scarcely less of a wonder that they should even be there at the start. This is a hopeful British entry by a group of professionals into what is almost exclusively the province of the Six, plus Spain and Switzerland.

There have been British teams in the race before, in 1955 (two finishers) and 1960 (three). But for the last five years there have only been the odd few British riders competing. In 1962, under pressure from the commercial sponsors, the Tour dropped the national divisions in favour of trade teams which rode under such flags as Peugeot-BP and Mann-Grundig.

But recently an equal and opposite pressure has been exerted by the French government. They are worried about the traffic chaos created by the Tour, for which the road ahead is closed for several hours. This may be tolerable in the pursuit of national glory, but not in the interest of petrol, motor-car and soft drink firms. So now the organisers have gone back to the old system.

The most respectable argument against it, anti-chauvinism apart, is based on the concentration of talent in a few countries. Belgium, for instance, had 40 riders in the last Tour. This year they have been allowed two 10-man teams; but that still leaves a score of good performers kicking their heels. Britain, Luxembourg and Switzerland, on the other hand, will have to include the odd scrubber to make up their numbers. Indeed, Britain would probably not have been accepted – as a single-nation team anyway – but for the presence on the Continent of one English rider undeniably of world class, Tom Simpson.

Simpson went to Brittany in 1959, a kind of Dick Whittington on export, with £100, an English bike and no French to speak of. He was so successful in local amateur races that at the end of the season St Raphael offered him a professional contract. With a lot of the showman about him, he made himself available to the press and played up his Englishness, making a name as the Major Thompson of the racing circuit.

At the same time he forced respect from the most cynical public any sport in the world has to cope with, by winning at least one of the classic races each season. He forces enormous effort from his tall, lean body: even French critics, who demand exceptional toughness from their heroes, talk of his foolish gluttony for work.

His prospects in the Tour will depend upon the quality of support he receives from the team (and perhaps some arrangements of mutual benefit he can make outside it).

CYCLISTS STOP RACE AS PROTEST

The Guardian, 30 June 1967

The Tour de France turned into a pantomime today when the cyclists stopped the race for three minutes a few miles outside Bordeaux, to protest against the new anti-doping measures. Dismounting from their bicycles, the competitors chanted derisively. This Rabelaisian scene was provoked by the anti-doping tests made the night before by doctors from the Ministry of Sport. It was the first time in the history of the race that such tests had been carried out. They are intended to enforce the legislation passed in France last year, and which has caused the withdrawal at the last minute of a number of Italian champions.

The first competitor to be tested was the second favourite, Raymond Poulidor. Poulidor said that he was taken completely unawares when he was confronted by police officer while being massaged after yesterday's stage. The officer showed his card and asked the cyclist to provide a urine sample. "I was flabbergasted," said Poulidor, "Emotions don't make these things any easier, you know." The tests are expected to become stricter when the mountain stages in the Pyrenees and the Alps are reached. The race will end in Paris on July 14, Bastille Day.

SIMPSON DIES AFTER COLLAPSE IN TOUR DE FRANCE

by Geoffrey Nicholson

The Guardian, 14 July 1967

CARPENTRAS, JULY 13

Tommy Simpson, the British cyclist, died early this evening after collapsing during a mountain stage of the Tour de France in intense heat this afternoon, on the ascent of Mont Ventoux, a barren mountain rising over 6,000ft near Carpentras.

A doctor tried to give him artificial respiration and he was flown at once by ambulance helicopter to Avignon hospital. But soon after 6.30 pm the press at Carpentras were told that Simpson, who was 29, had died. The collapse came two miles before the summit of Mont Ventoux on the thirteenth stage of the race from Marseilles to Carpentras. Simpson had been riding well through the day; all that struck one of his team mates was that he was taking drinks more often than usual. At the bottom of the Col he had been dropped by one of the leading groups, but towards the top of the climb he was still well up in the broken field and trying to regain contact with Aimar's small pursuing group 200 yards ahead.

FELL BY ROAD

Then, as the few eye witnesses described it, he faltered in his riding and fell over to the side of the road. The British team car was right behind him. Harry Hall, the team's chief mechanic, helped Simpson remount his cycle, but Simpson fell once more.

Dr Pierre Dumas, the doctor who travelled with the tour, examined him and immediately ordered his transfer by police helicopter to the nearest hospital. Simpson's was the first known death in the Tour's history. He was lying seventh in the overall race after the twelfth lap and was the only Briton ever to have worn the yellow jersey of overall leader in the race – in 1962. Tour officials announced that a ceremony to mark his death would be held tomorrow morning at the start of the fourteenth lap. "It is just like autoracing. The race goes on," said one.

The doctor who attended Simpson at the hospital refused to sign a burial certificate, which means that in all probability there will be a post-mortem examination.

As a rider Simpson was only just short of the very highest class. He was a good climber, a brave descender, an efficient all-rounder and highly professional. Only one season did he fail to win at least one of the classic races, and in 1965 he became world champion, and was voted sportsman of the year. But he was also impetuous and luck ran badly for him. He had frequent spills and a short time after winning the world championship he broke his leg in a skiing accident from which he took a full season to recover. He rode in five Tours de France before this one, but in the last two he was put out of the race through injury. He had badly wanted to do well this year to prove himself a reliable team man.

SIMPSON USED STIMULANTS

The Guardian, 4 August 1967

AVIGNON, AUGUST 3

It was officially confirmed today that the use of stimulants played a part in the death of the British racing cyclist, Tom Simpson, during the Tour de France on July 13. The official medical report, released today by the Avignon public prosecutor, said that Simpson, who was 29, died of heart failure due to exhaustion. "The unfavourable atmospheric conditions, intense overexertion and the use of dangerous medicines could have contributed to the exhaustion syndrome. Toxological experts confirmed that a certain quantity of amphetamine and methyl-amphetamine, substances making up in part the pharmaceutical products found in Simpson's clothing, have been discovered in his blood, urine, stomach content and intestines. These same experts confirm that the dose of amphetamine taken by Simpson would not have been enough, by itself, to kill Simpson, but would have permitted him to pass the limit of his endurance and thus allow him to fall victim to excessive exhaustion."

SNOW AND ICE STOPS TEN – BUT NOT VAN SPRINGEL

The Guardian, 9 July 1969

Hermann Van Springel, of Belgium, won the tenth stage of the Tour de France here today after the riders had fought their way through snow storms over some of the highest passes in the French Alps. Van Springel reached the top of the Col du Galibier (8,888ft) in a group with seven other riders, including most of the favourites. Then he sprinted away over the 21 miles to Briançon, and won by over two minutes. His time was not sufficient to make any difference to the main places overall, however, and Eddy Merckx (Belgium), a former world champion, retained the lead.

But if Van Springel made no impression on the top positions, today's gruelling ride, the snow, ice and freezing cold did. At least 10 men abandoned, among them the Belgian champion, Roger de Vlaeminck. The difficulties also caused Jan Janssen into second place last year, and Derek Harrison (Britain) to lose contact with the stage leaders – and their chances in the Tour. The weary Hoban, covered in mud, said that this Tour de France was the most difficult he had experienced.

MERCKX IS SUPREME

The Guardian, 21 July 1969

Eddy Merckx yesterday became the first Belgian in 30 years to win the Tour de France cycle classic. He underlined his dominance of this year's race by recording his sixth stage win in the final 22.8-mile time trial to Paris, taking his overall lead to 17min 54sec.. He swept into the Vincennes Velodrome to a rapturous welcome from the thousands of Belgians who had poured into Paris during the preceding 24 hours.

Merckx, on his return home to Belgium, will receive a royal welcome from his king in Brussels. And it is a welcome he deserves, for yesterday Merckx, in his first ever Tour de France, became the first man to win the overall points and mountain classifications.

Already Merckx is the highest-paid rider in the world, reputed to be earning £83,400 a year. Organisers of post-Tour races, where Tour winners really reap the benefit of their efforts, are offering up to £1,000 for a one-day appearance by Merckx.

CHAPTER FOUR
BREAKING BOUNDARIES

Is Merckx now riding for a fall?

THE TOUR DE FRANCE, which holds its time trial prologue in Charleroi, Belgium, tomorrow evening, comes more and more to resemble a Mohammed Ali title fight. The question is not so much who will win, but whether the champion — now making a detectable effort to achieve what need to come so easily — will at last be beaten.

So far Eddy Merckx has won all the five Tours de France he has entered, and it must seem capricious to look any further for this year's winner. But this big, dark

GEOFFREY NICHOLSON considers the pressures which the five-times winner of the Tour de France faces

Belgian with old-fashioned good looks — a muscular Tyrone Power — was at last week, and a number of rivals will be covertly looking for grey hairs.

He has said himself that he is over the col at a peak by classic rider, although if that's true he's coasting very nicely down the other side. In the past 12 months he has won his third professional road race title, the Milan-San

Remo, Tour of Flanders and Liège-Bastogne-Liège — hardly the record of a man who can no longer concentrate his effort into an hours' solid racing. Even in the Tour de France, where the sun is three weeks' consistency over mountains and plains, in sprints and time trials, rather than day-to-day victories. Merckx was able to win eight stages and right last year.

All the same, every kilometre more that Merckx has to ride shortens the odds on him faltering at some point along the way. This he did in the Alps two years ago, when Luis Ocaña took almost Merckx out of him, only to fall himself in the Pyrenees and retire from the race.

Certainly he is not as well prepared as usual. He had to withdraw from the Tour of Italy with tendinitis, and after convalescing, work his way gradually back into form that when his rivals were watching their peak. Without that explanation, why could imagine Merckx coming seventh in the time trial that opened the Tour of Switzerland a fortnight ago? but he did, and Roger de Vlaeminck, a fellow Belgian set in brotherly as Cain, was quick to snatch the advantage.

De Vlaeminck, who is also world cyclo-cross champion, would be more than willing to repeat that performance in the Tour de France. So would the Dutchman, Joop Zoetemelk, who for two years running has been Merckx in the Paris-Milan stage race, Ocaña, and a crew of Spanish climbers, and the French pair, Jean-Pierre Danguillaume and Bernard Thevenet, all know what it is to finish ahead of Merckx. It's never certain who will start the Tour until they attempt at the top of the race, for the time trial, but there will be at least not a dozen riders waiting for Merckx to drop his guard.

This pattern of the racing will surely change this June because, for the first time since 1967, there will be no time trials at the mountain passes. This experience is at least worth trying, for both the summary and the other spectacular effect on the early stages had quite made it again when refers to the value riders, however be bankrupt for the plains to neglect the trace stages. Independently with riders in the middle of the race.

The Tour still helps the problem of a series of mass sprint finishes in the first 10 days' sport riding on the best secateur riders and the mountains, France's break at the Midi Court — three mountains of days this week; help stage climbs from four destination. It's not the mountains of finishes with Nice in 1992, and these will be crucial.

Sean Kelly leads Irish challenge

Sean Kelly leads Irish challenge

By a Special Correspondent

English riders were relegated from the leading four positions in the strong Irish team made their mark in yesterday's Chessington Cycles senior amateur road race on the third day of the Harrogate international festival.

Victory went to their rider, Sean Kelly, the winner of the Southport-Southend stage of this year's Milk Race. He won comfortably from Sandy Gilchrist, of Scotland, after they had broken clear on the last four laps of a 15 mile circuit. At the line they were 17 seconds clear and in the sprint for third place the next two riders over the line were the Irish brothers, Pat and Ollie Richard, Dave Marsh and Gethin Smith, both riding for Oldham, and a second GB tractors' Invincible team, led home the English contingent.

Sid Barras (Barras) made some amends for his lack of success in Sunday's British professional Championship, when he won the professional event later this days of the same circuit. Barras, the country's most prolific winner in recent years, beat in a length ahead of Mick Bennett (Falcon Cycles). There two riders were just clear of the main with Barras's fastest team-mate bullfinish, taking the sprint for third place from Pat Locher (Holdsworth).

INTERNATIONAL

MERCKX DOES IT AGAIN

The Guardian, 20 July 1970

Eddy Merckx, of Belgium, crushed all opposition to win the Tour de France cycle race today for the second time in two years. Merckx won by almost 13 minutes from Joop Zoete-melk, of Holland, and more than a quarter of an hour clear of Sweden's Gosta Petterson, who was third.

Merckx emphasised the authority he has shown throughout the 23 days of the Tour with an astonishing win in the last stage, a 33.5-mile time trial from Versailles to the Vincennes Velodrome here. Merckx finished in 1hr 9min 39sec, 1min 47sec faster than Luis Ocana, of Spain, covering the course at more than 29 miles an hour.

Merckx's victory made him only the third man in cycling history to have won the Tour of Italy and the Tour de France in the same season. The feat was done twice by Fausto Coppi, of Italy, in 1949 and 1952 and once by Jacques Anquetil, of France, in 1964. Merckx's stage win today was the eighth of the Tour, equalling a record that has stood since 1937 by Guy Lapebie, of France. Merckx also shared in the win by his Italian supported team, Faemino, in the team trial stage.

Merckx said after the race that the last stage had been particularly dangerous because of the numerous sharp bends and the often wet road. "I was trembling at the start because I was so worried. I was frightened of falling – frightened of losing," Merckx said.

EDDY MERCKX EQUALS ANQUETIL'S RECORD

From a Special Correspondent
The Guardian, 24 July 1972

Eddy Merckx, the Belgian world champion, equalled Jacques Anquetil's record of four successive victories when he won the Tour de France cycle classic here today. The 27-year-old Belgian covered the 2,385 miles in 108 hours, 17 minutes, 18 seconds to finish nearly 11 minutes ahead of his nearest challenger, the 1965 champion Felice Gimondi of Italy. The French veteran Raymond Poulidor, competing in his tenth Tour, was third – 53 seconds behind Gimondi.

The incomparable Merckx also won the combined placings prize, based on points gained from the daily stage placings, and was second to the Belgian Lucien van Impe in the mountain section. Merckx sportingly handed over the green Jersey of the points prize winner to the Frenchman Cyrille Quimard, who was forced to retire with tendon trouble on Friday when he led the points category and was second overall to the Belgian.

It was Guimard's withdrawal, following the earlier retirement of the Spanish mountain specialist Luis Ocana with pneumonia, which virtually ended the three-week tour as a contest.

Yet Merckx still described this year's event as the most difficult of his four Tours. He was level headed after recovering the lead in the eighth of the 21 stages and had cracked second-placed Ocana by the end of the second week with his conquering rides in the Pyrenees and Alps.

Merckx now hopes to complete a record-breaking five successive wins next year, which would also equal Anquetil's unprecedented number of Tour victories. For Poulidor, at 33, it was probably his last chance of winning the Tour, after finishing second twice and third four times.

THE WAY THE WEST WAS WON

by Geoffrey Nicholson

The Observer, 30 June 1974

The first stage of the Tour de France ever run in Britain – a circuit race of just over 100 miles up and down the Plymouth by-pass – was also the first Tour win for new Dutch professional

Henk Poppe. It also brought his Frisol team a special bonus of £310 which their sponsors had offered that morning for a win here.

It was a remarkably astute piece of work for a rider who is not yet 22 and unused to this level of competition. The race was strongly controlled by Eddy Merckx and his Molteni team to prevent any breakaway, and was clearly going to end in a mass sprint.

From some words that passed, Poppe got the idea that Merckx was going to allow Patrick Sercu, a close friend, though in a rival team, to take the sprint. So at the end of the fourteenth and final lap, as the field swept down from road bridge to the finish, Poppe stuck to Sercu's back wheel and then came from behind to beat him on the line.

It was a surprise to everyone but the Dutch, who reckon Poppe to be the strongest – though not perhaps the fastest – sprinter in Europe. He was helped to use this strength by the head wind blowing up the final straight. So there was no move by Merckx, who remains second overall in the Tour to his team mate Bruyère, and no home victory for Barry Hoban. But Hoban had no reason to regret the visit for he had a first and a third place in the two intermediate Hot Spot sprints, which won him back 8 sec. in bonuses, and also left him third behind Merckx and Karstens on the Hot Spot points list. He also won a £100 sprint prize and ninth place on the stage.

Half-an-hour after the start the best guess that the police could make of the crowd was 15,000. The day brightened considerably after a misty start. The idly curious were rare. Nearly all the Devon accents came from the mouths of constables or men in Plymouth Corporation jerkins. As ever it was the faithful who made up the numbers.

They got pretty good value. They could recognise the past Tour winners: Merckx in the white jersey of points leader instead of the expected yellow, the tall but otherwise unobtrusive Pingeon who never looks quite well enough to be riding a bicycle – and shyly smiling Poulidor, almost as famous and rich for never winning the Tour.

There was an edited version of the publicity caravan with a pretty girl throwing Breton artichokes into the crowd, and more pretty girls on another lorry following up with buttons which said "I get fresh with Stella."

For a one-day show without the possibility of a dress rehearsal, the arrangements made by the Plymouth organisers were almost beyond reproach except, perhaps, for the number of people wandering around with press tickets who would have to chew their pencils before they even wrote their names. Alfred Palmer, the stage director, had not been to bed, and it was only at 5am, when the road was closed to traffic, that he was able to build the press stand from scratch and get the public address system wired up.

The fans got their money's worth but did the sponsor? While Plymouth put up £40,000 to provide the basic facilities, the Brittany growers – hence all those artichokes – spent £180,000 on the four stages in their region, which included the cost of transporting the race across the Channel. They may feel the small crowd support and the lack of television coverage didn't justify the cost.

Certainly the trip wasn't widely popular with the riders, mainly because they had to make two early starts to fit it in. Ideally they just like to ride eat and sleep. They couldn't complain about the warmth of their welcome from the hard-core British race followers, the warmth of the weather, or the arrangements for the race. We probably won't have to wait another 71 years for another British Tour de France stage – provided the price is right.

CONFIDENT HOBAN WINS STAGE

The Guardian, 12 July 1974

Barry Hoban of Britain, having his best season for many years at the age of 34, won yesterday's 13th stage of the Tour de France. Hoban just edged out the Tour's leading sprinters in a mass dash for the line at the end of the 78-mile run from Avignon. Hoban is having his best tour yet. From the start in Brest 15 days ago, he has dominated the world's top sprinters, finishing high in the flat stages and winning many of the intermediary sprints that mark each stage. So good has been his sprinting that he is now well clear at the top of the overall intermediary sprint placings, with a strong chance of the top prize in Paris in 10 days' time. The completely flat stage – one of the shortest of the tour – predictably made no difference to the overall placings and the Belgian Eddy Merckx still holds the lead, two minutes and one second ahead of Gonzalo Aja, of Spain.

DEATH THREAT TO TOUR CYCLISTS

The Guardian, 18 July 1974

Death threats were made against Spanish riders in the Tour de France cycle race today, and Spanish fencers were also threatened at the world championships in Grenoble. Spanish anarchists of the Internationalist Revolutionary Action Group

(GARI) told newspapers in the south-west of France by telephone that they were ready to go to any lengths to stop the two Spanish cyclists from reaching Paris.

Police watch on the Tour de France has been stepped up since bombs destroyed several cars accompanying the race at St Lary in the Pyrenees yesterday. The Spanish riders' hotel is kept under continual police watch and the Tour vehicles are also being closely protected. In the call to the newspaper *La Dépêchce du Midi*, a man saying he represented GARI said: "There will be several attacks before the Tour ends. Some of them may be fatal." The Spanish riders nevertheless started today's eighteenth stage.

MORNING GLORY

by Geoffrey Nicholson
The Observer, 21 July 1974

Eddy Merckx may be the best man in the house, but he cannot believe he has proved it until everyone else is left groaning on the floor. So by his own combative standards, today's split stage in the Tour de France, on the eve of the finish in Paris tomorrow, was only a partial success.

This phenomenal Belgian rider, with the dark looks of a silent movie star and the build of an English centre three-quarter, won the morning's 70-mile road race between Vouvray and Orléans. This was the section which he was expected to leave as a tip for lesser riders now that he has the greater prize of the race itself in his pocket.

Five hours later he was beaten in the 23 and a half-mile time trial – an event in which he is the acknowledged master – by an ambitious young Belgian from a rival team, Michel Pollentier. If the morning brought him his seventh win of the tour, the afternoon cost him the chance of equalling Charles Pélissier's 1930 record of eight stage wins, and perhaps beating it tomorrow. To someone like Merckx, that is a failure to brood on.

If there was a derisive lack of sympathy for him from the French crowd, who have always thought him too avaricious, there was an overpowering warmth of feeling for their hero, Raymond Poulidor, who did not disappoint them. He came fifth in the trial with a time which was 2min 17sec, better than that of the Spanish champion, López Carril, and so by a single second jumped above him into second place overall behind Merckx.

The morning's route lay along the Loire, always radiant in the posters, but now filled with a thick drizzle which would have been more at home in the Rhondda. The racing was almost as colourless, despite its average speed of 30mph, and with six miles to go, Merckx became impatient with the inactivity. Pushing up his own pace to 37mph, he just left the field to their own devices and came in alone with lead of 1min 25sec.

Heading the bunch sprint, Patrick Sercu, the Belgian leader on points, again beat off the belligerent challenge from Barry Hoban, once of Wakefield, now of Ghent. But Hoban's third on the stage was sufficient to lift him into the same place overall in the points competition at the expense of Karstens, who fell at a roundabout about 150 yards out. This is the best position achieved in the points race by British rider.

EDDY MERCKX CONFIRMS HIS SUPERIORITY

by Geoffrey Nicholson
The Guardian, 22 July 1974

With the sun gleaming, and not for a moment in danger of setting on Eddy Merckx's yellow jersey, the sixty-first Tour de France moved 146 kilometres on from Orléans to its finish in Paris on the Piste Municipale du Bois de Vincennes. The scene at the roadside was like the Brighton promenade on a fine bank holiday, but stretching into infinity, and the "Cipale", the Continent's best-known outdoor cycling track, was filled by the promise of just 700 metres of sprinting.

What had brought out the crowds was not the inevitable victory of Merckx, even though he was equalling Jacques Anquetil's record of five Tour wins. It was the probability, balanced by one second in his favour, that their favourite, Raymond Poulidor, would finish second overall for the third time in his 12 tours. He had won this second advantage on López Carril in a 37.5-kilometre time trial on Saturday, and from the repeated messages of "Vive Poulidor" and "Merci, Pou-Pou" painted on the roadway and scrawled on cardboard placards you would have thought he had won race.

French enthusiasts cannot find Merckx, any more than they could Anquetil, really sympathetic, although they can never fail to respect a Tour winner. France turned the Tour into a unique test of endurance, and so they cannot believe that the man in the yellow jersey can be anything less than a giant. All the same French women, who make up a great percentage of those who watch and wait beside the road, complain that he lacks grace, and is too obviously ambitious.

The hard core of critics either criticise him for stifling the race and destroying the initiative of his rivals or, when he attacks and lays himself open to reprisal, say that he is greedy for honours and prizes. He is aware of these feelings, and reacts to them, but he cannot alter his basic competitive nature, or throw away his natural prudence.

CROWD PROVIDE MOST OF ACTION

by Geoffrey Nicholson

The Observer, 1 July 1975

Except in the mountains, where everything is played through in slow motion, the most that the spectators see on the Tour de France itself, not counting the cavalcade, is 10 seconds' blur of colour. It is radio, television and the press which provide the other five hours of the story, build up its epic qualities and create the heroes.

Yet on a bright Monday afternoon about 80,000 turned up to overflow the stands and terraces here. At least they saw the blur three times, for after crossing the finishing line the riders raced two laps of the 4 and a half-km Bugati circuit before Jacques Esclassan, one of Thévenet's men, gave them their first French stage win. They saw the Belgian points leader Rik van Linden crash as he finished second over the line and lost control of his machine. They then swarmed over the barriers and joined in the national pastime of trying to snatch the riders' cotton racing caps as souvenirs.

For 20 minutes there was chaos as the ambulance cut a passage through to the unlucky van Linden and riders forced their way to the team cars, sometimes carrying their bikes above their heads. It was not a very decisive stage – nothing was changed overall – but the Le Mans crowd saw, and contributed to, the most eventful part of it.

PARISIANS GO OUT ON HEAVENLY SPREE

Geoffrey Nicholson
The Guardian, 21 July 1975

The Tour de France could not have had a more grandiose ending than on the Champs-Élysées this afternoon when the French winner, Bernard Thévenet, and the defeated favourite, Eddy Merckx, stood on either side of president Giscard d'Estaing on the podium. The sun shone. The Marseillaise drowned the chanting of the demonstrators from the striking workforce of the *Parisien Libéré*.

The one "wasp at the picnic" – which prevented the whole thing becoming, as someone sourly described it, a festival – was that Walter Godefroot, a Belgian, won the final 163-km stage.

It was remarkable to see the famous avenue, the most urbane city main street in the world, turned into a criterium circuit. Normally stuffy restaurants had waiters dressed in racing jerseys selling sandwiches from their terraces and advertising special Tour de France menus – trade following the flag again. All along the route people stood half-a-dozen deep on the pavements, some reduced to the ultimate frustration of watching a cycle race through five-franc cardboard periscopes. And although the organisation had hoped to keep a 300-metre stretch along the Quai des Tuileries clear so that the riders could relieve themselves in privacy as they passed, the crowds were thick even there and put up with the embarrassment.

Whether or not the stage attracted the anticipated million spectators can only be guessed at, but the arrival of the president, "the most solemn moment of the Tour", as the commentators put it – and the presence of perhaps 200 demonstrators – certainly drew a force of 10,200 police of various orders. The demonstration was not reduced to silence, but was successfully sealed off from the eyes of the television.

The circuit ran anti-clockwise round the Champs-Élysées, starting from opposite the Elysée Palace, crossing the Rond Point, and moving on towards the Arc de Triomphe, a climb stiff enough to get attacking riders out of their saddle. Just short of Place Charles de Gaulle it turned, came back down the other side and circled the garden of the Tuileries to reach the finishing line again. In all, 27 laps of just over six kilometres were completed.

On the first lap Merckx and Thévenet were seen to attack together, but this was for the sake of the photographers and the crowds, and they soon settled back to leave the race to those seeking consolation prizes for their unrewarded efforts in the past three weeks. There was prize of 100 livres for the first man across the line at the end of every lap and points to the first five which would count to overall prizes of 250, 100, and 50 livres at the finish. Don Allen, who had managed to shed his last place in the race on Saturday's stage, was the first to break away alone and take two successive prizes.

In the past week Thévenet has emerged with a much more distinctive character, and if his nature is not naturally nice, the press has been determined to present him as a simple country Cinderella with a bicycle instead of a golden coach. There have been stories of his father's resistance to his making a career of cycling because it offered no future, and photographs of his parents on the 10-hectare farm they inherited from the family – a small peasant holding with four goats and 20 cows. The essential simplicity of his character is the thing. What is more uncertain is whether Thévenet's win was the culmination of gradually improving talent – or whether it resulted more from the curious terrain of this tour and Merckx's marginal lack of form. He has stubbornness, but has he the adaptable all-round ability of Merckx? France have their champion at last, but they must wait to see whether they have the durable "super champion" they have been seeking.

THIS PRIVATE PASSING SHOW

Hugh McIlvaney on the elusive qualities of the Tour de France, an
event seen by millions but only fleetingly
The Observer, 10 July 1977

Nothing about the Tour de France impresses more than its privacy. Following its progress at first-hand is, even with all the co-operation eagerly granted to the journalists and television crews, a physical impossibility. The millions who line the 2,500 miles of its great loop through half a dozen countries expect and receive no more than a blurred glimpse of bright jerseys, glittering spokes, and faces that are either drawn and sweaty on the days of attack and counter-attack or improbably relaxed when the field have conspired tacitly to defuse a stage and ride its length in a closely packed bunch, unaggressive as tourists.

As the Tour scudded or idled through the villages of France and northern Spain last week, the farmworkers by the roadside applauded and the priests in their dusty cassocks tried to identify the numbers on the leaders, but the reward of a long wait in the sun was simply the right to say they had seen it pass. Their attitude was not that of spectators at a sports event but of the crowds along the path of a State (or perhaps a religious) procession.

The reporters had a different attitude, but not much more of a view. They chased along in complaining cars, driving in a style that is rarely seen outside the Place de la Concorde or Hyde Park Corner, and most of the time they found themselves looking at nothing more informative than the damp shirt of a police motorcyclist up ahead.

At first such enforced remoteness is disturbing to someone accustomed to the press box at Cup Final or the ringside at a championship fight.

But before long the mind adjusts to the essential uniqueness of the Tour. Its dramas are not so much witnessed as absorbed and its story cannot be rendered or understood as a succinct and rounded narrative, only as a living accumulation of folklore over the 22 days of its duration. Its proper tradition of reporting is by word-of-mouth, tales brought back from a shifting battlefield.

The Tour, in spite of the mercenary values that pervade and often corrupt it, is immutably romantic because the people like it that way. And so, at the end of the day, do the riders.

Not all of them feel as deeply as the man who reverently buried his bike after winning, but all regard it as something much more than an access to better contracts. Those who win, or even those like Raymond Poulidor, who try memorably, can never be insignificant again.

Jean Robic's victory in the first of the post-war races in 1947 was rather freakish in that he never led until slipping deceptively and decisively clear of the more fancied competitors on the last stage. But the yellow jersey he wore then has been a kind of benevolent Shirt of Nessus and some measure of celebrity still clings to him. He is assumed to live in modest obscurity throughout the rest of the year but when he turns up at the Tour, as he has done this time, a marvellous shabby little man with a cigarette constantly bobbing all round his face that might be seen in a betting shop in Liverpool or Merthyr Tydfil, he is pointed out as an historic figure.

"He is a Hobbit," someone in our company said last week. The laughter was loud enough but it was kept the right side of respect by the memory of what that strange little man had done in his high summer 30 years ago.

If it requires an effort of the imagination to identify Jean Robic with glory, no such difficulty occurs with the supreme heroes of the Tour like Eddy Merckx. Anyone who saw Merckx in a hotel lobby or shopping in a supermarket would be likely to sense the presence of an extraordinary man. His handsome face, with the lips pursed and the eyes shadowed by preoccupation, conveys an assurance and strength that tells you this is someone who is used to betting himself for high stakes and rarely losing.

The romanticism that impregnates the event makes it natural that there should be an enthusiastic coining of nicknames; natural too that Merckx should be called 'the Cannibal' because of his capacity for devouring the hearts of opponents (not to mention team-mates). Jacques Anquetil, who, like Merckx, had five Tour victories, was a master of time trials and known as Monsieur le Chrono. Federico Bahamontes, a Spaniard who was superb in the mountains, was the Eagle of Toledo. Charly Gaul from Luxembourg also climbed magnificently, but with a light, feathery action, so they called him the Angel of the Mountains. Another performer was the Pedaller of Charm, for reasons that need not be inquired into.

The extravagant lyricism of such names is true to the feeling of the Tour. It has gathered a rich mythology since its beginnings more than 70 years ago: stories of triumph and calamity, of suicide and disintegration as well as glorious fulfilment. They are adding another chapter over in northern France this weekend. Don't fret if you cannot watch it take shape. The best of the stories will survive and, like all worthwhile legends, grow stronger with each retelling.

VIVE LE THÉVENET

by Philip Liggett

The Guardian, 25 July 1977

Bernard Thévenet of France celebrated his second Tour de France win in two years when the marathon ended its 4,100 kilometres on the Champs-Élysées yesterday. He preserved his lead on the two final stages, even slightly increasing it to 48 seconds in the time trial over TI Raleigh's Hennie Kuiper.

But while it was a day of French triumph it was also a day of shame, for this great race was again smeared by positive dope tests, and four more riders – 1973 winner Luis Ocana, Antoine Menendez and Fernando Mendez, all from Spain, and Portugal's Joaquim Agostinho – joined Saturday's announcement that pre-race favourite Joop Zoetemelk (Holland) and, before him, Spain's Sebastián Pozo had also taken forbidden stimulants.

The penalty for a first offence in cycling is one month's suspension; a 1,000 Swiss francs fine; 10 minutes' penalty; and last place on the stage. This means that Agostinho is disqualified from his win on the 18th stage and so is second-placed rider Menendez, as this was the stage when the latest tests proved positive.

Normally five tests are made each day, collated from the first and second riders on the stage, two at random and the overall leader.

The stimulant found in Zoetemelk's test was pemoline and he said on Saturday evening: "I know what people will say but swear I have taken nothing. That is why I wanted to win today so that I could take another test and prove it."

The race itself has been a great triumph for British machinery and the TI Raleigh team has won eight of the stages, held the race lead for 17 days, and won the team award.

THE WHEELER DEALERS
TWO YEARS AGO HARDLY ANYBODY ON THE CYCLE-MAD CONTINENT HAD HEARD OF BRITAIN'S RALEIGH BICYCLES. THEN RALEIGH WON THE TOUR DE FRANCE AND NOW EVERYBODY WANTS TO KNOW

Richard Yallop reports from the Biarritz stage
The Guardian, 15 July 1978

The Tour de France is big business. It is like a mile-long mobile billboard. It is costing £1.5 millions to stage this year and most of that is recouped from the advertisers and sponsors who proclaim their wares the length of the Tour. It provides them with an extraordinary opportunity to get their products known in France and throughout Europe. Back in 1974, that was realised by an astute marketing man at TI Raleigh, the English cycle company taken over by Tube Investments in the sixties.

Everyone in England knows Raleigh sell bikes, as do a fair number in America and the old Commonwealth countries, but in Europe few people had ever heard of them. Raleigh decided they would build a racing team which would one day win the Tour de France and make them known to every bike racer and cycle shop owner in Europe.

Last year they achieved their target of winning the team prize one year ahead of schedule. This year they hope for a repeat performance, having been joined by a further sponsor, McGregor, the sportswear manufacturers: so scattered among the bunch entering Biarritz were ten riders in the red, orange and black colours of TI Raleigh McGregor – six Dutch, three Belgians, and one West German. Riding behind in the team car was their Dutch manager Peter Post, the man chosen by Raleigh in 1974 to lead the team. It was a good day for Raleigh, with two men in the first six. Raleigh hoped to achieve their success with a team largely composed of English riders, and the team Post began with in 1974 had 12 Englishmen and six foreigners. England, however, has still to take to cycling as a major spectator sport and consequently the number of high-quality riders who choose to make it their profession has always been small. Post went by results, and as the English rarely got any, they gradually left the team. Bill Nickson was the last to leave, in March this year.

Sunday was supposed to be a rest day for the Raleigh team. They trained in the morning and then went on display at a free lunch given by Raleigh for the press. While the more conscientious reporters arranged interviews, the rest sat on the hotel terrace overlooking the ranks of sunbathers down on the Grande Plage. Raleigh lay on another of these do's when the Tour reaches Paris, and they provide coffee and rum for the press at the beginning and end of each stage. They have discovered the way to a journalist's heart is via his stomach.

Raleigh's budget for the Tour is £35,000 of which £14,000 is the entry fee for the race, which includes rooms for the night en route. Their entire racing budget for 1978 is £400,000, which brings the total spent on the team since it was founded in 1974 to £1 million. The cash is beginning to show a return. European sales rose by 30 per cent last year after their Tour win, and the Paris cycle show alone, coming two months after their win, brought in 600 new dealers. Previously France had been a closed shop. Other markets opened up in Italy and Norway, and their share rose in Holland and Belgium. In November and December production at the Nottingham factory ceased for six weeks over a pay dispute, but even so sales in 1978 are likely to be up by 25 per cent.

Post and the riders are well aware they are engaged in public relations. Interview appointments stretched out all afternoon. Post was besieged by Dutch television and radio crews. He is a tall, imposing man, immaculately turned out in matching blue Raleigh shirt and trousers and sunglasses. He was supreme in six-day track racing when he rode professionally in the sixties. Nobody has ever matched his record of 65 six-day wins.

It is said the Raleigh riders are Post's soft spot. He ensures they have the best food and the best hotels, and in return he expects them to be Raleigh men 24 hours day. They eat in their track suits, attend functions in blue safari suits, and relax in public in matching blue cotton shirts and shorts. Self-discipline is the team rule. Post expects complete dedication. He once complained about the lack of single-mindedness of one of the team (who has since left), "Every night he rings his girl friend. That should be his girlfriend," and he pointed to one of the team bikes. He is currently casting covetous eyes at a rider in another team, who satisfies all Post's requirements for the perfect professional. "He thinks only of his bicycle, his bed, and his food," said Post.

Cycle racing requires an astute tactical mind. Like chess it has its kings and it has its pawns. Hennie Kuiper, the team's Dutch captain, is Raleigh's king, the rider the other teams must capture if their own king is to prevail. His room mate, the Belgian Jos de Cauwer, is pawn. In cycling they call the pawns *domestiques* – servants. They will ride ahead to bear the force of the wind, sacrifice their wheel if their leader punctures away from the team car, and pace him back into the main bunch of riders if he's had a spare wheel supplied by the team car.

TOUR DE FARCE

by Geoffrey Nicholson
The Observer, 23 July 1978

Most years the Tour de France is like one of those big, untidy Victorian novels which suffer from having first appeared as a magazine serial ... the early instalments are slow and pretty uneventful. In fact they could be cut from the plot completely except that the public demands a good, long read and the authors have to make a crust. It's not until halfway through that the true hero reveals himself. At which point, with several chapters left to be completed, he prematurely makes good and the rest is anticlimax. Or else he is arbitrarily killed off, and the ending has to be botched together with a new set of leading characters. The whole thing is strong on action and atmosphere, but decidedly weak in dramatic construction.

This is where the 1978 Tour has differed. The plot has been masterly, even though, in the final week, a cruder, more melodramatic hand has been at work. Last Sunday's stage from St Etienne to Alpe d'Huez was well up to narrative standard. Still in the yellow jersey was Joseph Bruyère, the reticent troubleshooter for Eddy Merckx until he was given his head by the great man's retirement in the spring. Of the five dogs who had their day in the opening stages Bruyère was the bravest and most tenacious, but on the Col du Luitel he finally declined and the real favourites took over the running.

First to the top of the Luitel, and down the sinuous descent towards the final climb, went another Belgian, Michel Pollentier, and after him chased a posse of all who had any credible ambition to win the Tour. Alpe d'Huez is a 14-kilometre staircase rising 1,000 metres in 21 hairpin bends, and as Paul Sherwen, riding his first Tour put it, not at all like his own Frodsham Hill. Fighting his bike all the way up, Pollentier managed to keep 38 seconds clear, and with the help of a time bonus took the overall lead. But only by a margin that left him teetering on the peak. The tall, thoughtful, perhaps too thoughtful, Dutchman Joop Zoetemelk, never a Tour winner but three times runner-up, was just four seconds behind. Bernard Hinault, the young Breton whom the French see as their next champion, was at 18 seconds, and the rest of the Alpine stages were to come.

It was two hours later that the first ominous note sounded. An announcement was made at the press room in the nave of our Lady of the Snows – a nice touch – that Pollentier had not presented himself at the dope control. The doctor was looking for him.

Then came the communiqué which turned the acceptable suspense story into something closer to black comedy. For defrauding the control, the man who had only just put on the yellow jersey was banished from the Tour, fined 5,000 Swiss francs (about £1,200), and suspended from racing for two months, which would cost him all his lucrative post-Tour contracts to appear in one-day events in Belgium and France.

What Pollentier had done was to conceal a rubber bulb containing someone else's urine under his arm. From this a rubber tube was wound around his body with the end hidden beneath his shorts. The device was discovered by a conscientious doctor in charge of the control for the first time, who insisted on applying the international rules. These say that a rider giving a urine sample must be bared from the knees to above the waist.

In fact the good doctor found three malefactors among the six he tested, for Antoine Gutierrez was also caught in fraud, and José Nazabal gave a genuine sample which proved positive. That night, and much of the following rest day at the ski resort, were spent turning up for conferences with the management of Pollentier's Flandria team, regularly promised and just as regularly postponed. At last, early on the Monday afternoon, groups of reporters were allowed to file through Pollentier's hotel bedroom and onto his balcony. There, against an aseptic background of snowy mountain tops, Pollentier, switching between French, German, Flemish and English, put his side of a murkier scene.

He is a courteous, sympathetic man of 27 with a pale, thin face below thinning fair hair. A professional of consequence for several years, he was understandably distressed to find himself in this humiliating position.

With surprising candour he admitted using the apparatus and having taken a branded preparation "for the breathing". He said it was permitted in Italian racing, but because he didn't know whether or not it was on the international list of forbidden substances, he had been prepared to evade the control. His grievances were that at least 50 per cent of the riders were using products – "I'm not saying they are drugs" – that previous controls in the Tour were far more lenient, and that one rider, whom he named, had deliberately taken third place on a stage because only the first two were automatically tested. "They were looking for me", he said, "because they want me out of the race."

This answered a few serious questions but raised enough, some English and Danish reporters felt, to need an answer from the organisers. Jaques Goddet, one of the two race directors, is a distinguished, high-minded man in his early seventies who in many ways embodies the spirit and conscience of the Tour. He agreed that there might be variations in the procedure at the controls, since they are carried out by different doctors, but while he deplored the scandal, the organisers were only the executives of the Tour: the Union Cycliste Internationale were the legislative authority and it was up to them to tighten up the regulations.

Which is true, of course. But the naive clumsiness of the attempted frauds shows the contempt in which riders hold dope controls. And if the Tour can do no more than ask the UCI to apply its rules more strictly, perhaps it's time the sponsors took a hand. They could well copy the example of Raleigh, who have a break-clause in their riders' contracts which comes into force if they fall foul of the doping laws.

FUGITIVES ON WHEELS

by Frank Keating

The Guardian, 7 July 1979

It was good news for the cycling nuts – and few sportsmen are nuttier than cyclists – that ITV's *World of Sport* is again covering the Tour de France. Beggars can't be choosers, and even if a 12-minute summary of the Tour each Saturday is meagre fare, well it's better than nothing.

In the middle 1960s the Tour passed through a nearby village when I was staying in the Dordogne Valley. Suddenly an enthralling, near-absurd spectacle was on us. Just as suddenly it was gone. Geoffrey Nicholson once said that the first time you came across the Tour is was "like witnessing the Second Coming from the top of passing bus". Exactly.

I fancy it cannot have changed since *Le Matin* sent Collette to cover a stage 67 years ago: "I saw three slight riders pass in front of us, to be immediately swallowed up in swirls of dust: black and yellow backs with red numbering, the three might just as well have been faceless, their heads down around their knees, their spines in an arch ... Very quickly they vanished, the only quiet people in all the uproar; both their haste in pushing on and their silence seemed to cut them off from all that was happening around.

"One would not say that they are competing with one another so much as that they are fleeing us, they who are the quarry of this escort among which one finds, all swirled together in the turbid dust, screams, horn-blowings, cheering, and the rolling of thunder."

Cycle-racing, appropriately, was pioneered in France. The first cycle race took place at the Parc de St Cloud in Paris, in 1868; it was over 1,312 yards and was won by an English resident, James Moore. The first inter-town road race, between Paris and Rouen, followed 18 months later, Moore again winning, covering 83 miles in 10 and a half hours.

This year's is the 76th Tour. The first Paris–Marseilles–Toulouse–Bordeaux–Paris trip was sponsored by a sports magazine. Cheats prospered: the leaders dropped handfuls of nails from their saddlebags; some riders took the train; some were poisoned. But gradually the race flourished into nothing less than a phenomenon, much due to the organising genius and fervour of Henri Desgrange.

For the start in 1911, for instance, he read from the pulpit his legendary "Acte d'adoration pour le Tour": "Today, my brothers, we gather in common celebration of the divine bicycle. Not only do we owe it our most pious gratitude for the precious and ineffable love it has given us, but also for the host of memories sown and which today has made concrete.

In my own case I love it for its having given me a soul capable of appreciating it. I love it for having taken my heart within its spokes, for having encircled part of my life within its harmonious frame, and for having constantly illuminated me with the victorious sparkle of its nickel plates. In the history of humanity does it not constitute the first successful effort of intelligent life to triumph over the laws of weight?"

The religious flavours for cyclists and their grandest tour prevail. Tommy Simpson, the English rider who died, drugged in the mountains in 1967, is not considered a tragically misguided young man by the pedalling fraternity but a martyr to the great cause who had simply fallen bravely in a pitiless event of grandeur. Even today, I am told, hundreds of pilgrims annually travel to pay respect at Simpson's grave in Halworth, Nottinghamshire.

Since that unforgettable morning when the incredible caravan whooshed through my holiday village, I have been determined to one day wangle a trip to the Tour. Alas, now another year has gone by ... not, mind you, that I'm pretending I really understand what is going on. In his lovely book *The Great Bike Race*, published by Hodder last year, Geoff Nicholson tried to explain his fascination: "Riders do not just put heads down and their bottoms up and pelt from A to B; they attack and chase, flag and rally, form instant alliances for immediate ends, and then break them without another thought." Even more compelling, though, was the strong narrative quality of the sport. A race was a rounded, self-contained story with complex relationships, sudden shifts of action, identifiable heroes, a beginning, middle and end. When it was a stage in a longer race, then it became another chapter in a picaresque novel which each day introduced new characters in a different setting.

FARM BOY REAPING RICH HARVEST

Geoffrey Nicholson reports on a slow-mannered countryman with one of the fastest finishes in the Tour de France
The Observer, 22 July 1979

Rider No 106, who competes in the colours of Splendor-Euro-soap, has the traditional background of a French professional cyclist. He was born and brought up on a 50-acre dairy farm, one of three sons of a Catholic family. His talent for the sport was spotted at school, which he left early to help on the farm and work as a brickie's labourer. At 17 he first rode as an international in the European Youth Rally, and at 20, after a successful year with the Velo Club Metz – during which he won 15 races, including one amateur classic, the Tour of Lombardy – he was offered a professional contract by the

Belgian team, Flandria. He is a slow, big-boned lad, 1 metre 75 tall and 68 kilogrammes, with the slow, careful manner of the countryside. With it, too, an acceptance of discomfort and a contempt for minor injury.

What sets him apart is that the farm where he was born is in Carrick-on-Suir, County Tipperary, and while a French boy with a precocious gift for cycling would have been programmed by his local club for a professional career, Sean Kelly almost blundered into it.

At 18, tieless, suitless, and looking very much out of his world until he sat on a bicycle, he quickly adapted from the 40-mile courses of Irish cycling to the 100-mile stages of the British Milk Race. As the youngest rider, he was lying third overall on the final stage when a puncture and a slow wheel-change sent him tumbling down the table. All the same, it was a remarkable opening, and Kelly seemed certain to ride for Ireland in the 1976 Olympics. Instead, that autumn his career took one of those haphazard lurches which generally seem to work out in his favour. He rode in an invitation race in South Africa, the Rapport Tour, and when the news leaked out he was banned by the Irish Olympic Committee.

Having nothing to do after the 1976 Milk Race, he accepted an offer to spend the rest of the summer with VC Metz, something of a twin town for British cyclists. He still thought no further than getting his amateur riding subsidised, but after he had won the Tour of Lombardy, the trade teams began to do his thinking for him.

Back in Carrick at the end of the season he got a telephone call from William Driessens, manager of Flandria, offering him a £6,000 professional contract. Kelly, thinking he had said £600, considered a moment, then turned him down. But that again worked out for the best. The astonished Driessens came in person to Carrick with revised terms and, this time with no change of expression, Kelly settled for £9,000.

So began two seasons with Flandria. In 1977 he earned his crust by coming second in the Tour of Holland. Last year he first rode, and at Poitiers won a stage, in the Tour de France. His main job was to lead out the phenomenal Freddy Maertens, winner of 11 Tour stages, in the sprints, forcing a passage through the bumping, boring mass, then moving aside so that Maertens could streak away from his rear wheel.

It was a privileged apprenticeship, as Kelly admits: "He is the best finishing sprinter I have ever seen." And the experience of devilling for Maertens took Kelly into all the bunch finishes where he could absorb the tactics and file away the peculiarities of the other sprinters. But after two years Kelly wanted to be the protected sprinter himself, and Splendor (who make the bikes – Eurosoap are the moneybags) offered that chance at a big jump in salary.

He is now on roughly £15,000 – a good wage by Belgian standards – which he probably more than doubles through winnings and appearance money at criteriums. Not that Kelly talks about that. He has a farm boy's closeness on a subject as intimate as money.

This season began with typical confusion, both Flandria and Splendor claiming Kelly as their own. Kelly admits that had he known Maertens would pull out with "physical exhaustion" he might have stayed with Flandria. Last week he was one of only two survivors of the original 10, and all that kept them plugging on was the hope that Kelly might win one of the late flat stages. But the odds were long. One helper was not enough to oppose the strong red guard of Flandria, working away to lead out Demeyer.

In some ways Kelly, still only 23 after all, seemed lost. An Irish cycling official over here on holiday said he was surprised to find Kelly talking to him in "Pidgin English – a rough translation" of the basic French he habitually speaks in which one verb – "make" – serves every purpose. Kelly makes races, makes training, makes interviews, makes practically everything.

But while he articulates his thoughts with difficulty, and a great many shrugging, twisting gestures, he keeps his native shrewdness. And all the while he is developing his one special and highly saleable talent: his ability, after racing 120, miles to jump ahead of the finishing sprint.

Given proper support – which he now hopes to find in a rebuilt Splendor team rather than in a rumoured move to Paul Sherwen's Fiat – he could enjoy a few golden summers as the game's top sprinter on the road.

And although land in Southern Ireland "is getting terribly expensive", by the time he is in his early thirties he could be back there farming a good deal more than 50 acres of it.

HINAULT'S GOLDEN ROAD

Phil Liggett

The Guardian, 24 July 1979

The price of fame is rising comfortably for the formidable Bernard Hinault, who won his second Tour de France last Sunday. Yesterday he picked up £4,000 for simply starting in two small-town races in his native Brittany. These criteriums – and Hinault has signed to race in 23 of them during the next month at upwards of £2,000 an appearance – are the true paydays for a successful rider.

Hinault's nine Tour de France team mates were totally committed to his success, or failure, and are also all the richer for their loyalty. As a sign of appreciation Hinault did not keep a franc of his £100,000 winner's prize nor, it is said, any of the £45,000 his Renault team won during their 24-day, 3700-kilometre trek around France with incursions to Switzerland, Spain and Belgium.

He did not, of course, donate his unrevealed, but certainly hefty, bonus from the car company who on Sunday proudly renamed Le Pub Renault on the Champs-Élysées as Le Pub Hinault.

The Breton, still only 24, this year proved that he combines the strength of the great Belgian Eddy Merckx, the time-trial skills of Jacques Anquetil and the businesslike approach to the sport which has become his trademark.

CHAPTER FIVE
THE AMERICANS ARRIVE

Geoffrey Nicholson in Basle previews the Tour de France

Swiss roll out red carpet

🕐 CYCLING

Over the years Switzerland has contributed about as much to the Tour de France as it has to military strategy or women's suffrage. In fact only two Swiss names, Kubler and Koblet, chime out from the records with any resonance—they won the race consecutively in 1950-51. But this afternoon, for the very first time, the Tour will start in Switzerland with a 7.4km time trial prologue in the suburbs of Basle.

What brought the Tour here, for once, was charity. Over the past 10 years a group of sportsmen in the region have raised six million Swiss francs—roughly £1.7 million—on behalf of deprived children, in particular the Pestalozzi orphans' village.

As a final fling in their campaign they formed a committee to sponsor the prologue of the Tour and tomorrow's opening stage on a road circuit 25km from Basle. Although this will cost them one million Swiss francs, they hope to raise as much again for the children over the weekend.

Backing up the effort, the Swiss have entered 17 riders in the field of 170, both of which are record figures. Even in the days of national teams, the Swiss never had more than 10 in the race. As for the grand total of starters, which threatens early congestion and crashes, this beats the previous highest in 1928 when 162 riders set out from Paris but only 41 returned.

Apart from the Swiss entry, what has helped to swell the numbers is the return of the Italians after a couple of years' absence. They have two 10-man teams and at least two riders who might stir up trouble in the mountains, the experienced Giovanni Battaglin and another good climber, Mario Beccia. Yet although he may find himself harder pressed it is the Frenchman, Bernard Hinault, who is again favourite to win.

Hinault is certainly not a man to dissipate his talents. Like a racehorse he treats certain events as training rides, and he cannot feasibly reach the number of classic and stage-race victories achieved by the Belgian, Eddy Merckx. But having just won the Giro d'Italia, he could earn a place alongside Merckx, Fausto Coppi and Jacques Anquetil as only the fourth man to take both the Italian and French Tours in the same year.

There is also still the chance that in the Tour de France,

where both his pride and his abilities are best expressed, he could outshine Merckx and Anquetil. Each won five Tours to tie the record before retiring; Hinault has won three. Since Hinault is only 27, and with his powers seemingly unimpaired when he chooses to exercise them, there is no self-evident reason why he should not win his sixth Tour before he is 30.

If this is the biggest Tour yet, it is also, at 3,830km, the shortest since the second in 1904. This will not greatly help

Hinault, who is essentially an endurance rider. Nor will the particular clockwise route which the Tour takes this year, after the Ballon d'Alsace on Sunday there will be no climbing of any significance until the Tour reaches the Pyrenees 10 stages later. With only moderate team support, Hinault will find it hard to dominate the racing over a succession of flat stages.

There he will have the company of Lucien van Impe, last year's king of the mountains, who has broken a rib. Another Belgian absentee is Freddy Maertens, who went on from winning the points competition in the Tour to take the world championship in Prague but has been dropped for loss of form.

The English-speaking contingent, however, is up to strength. Paul Sherwen of Frodsham is back for the fifth time; so is the Irish sprinter, Sean Kelly. The Australian Phil Anderson and the American Jonathan Boyer ride their second tours. Although that other dogged English rider, Graham Jones, has missed selection, a New Zealander, Eric McKenzie, makes up the numbers.

THE TOUR GOES DUTCH

by Phil Liggett

The Guardian, 21 July 1980

Joop Zoetemelk of Holland gave the TI-Raleigh-Creda team victory at last in the Tour de France, which ended on the Champs-Élysées in Paris yesterday. The final 118 miles, a loop around the Chevreuse Valley from Fontenay-sous-Bois, a Paris suburb, proved to be a formality for the Dutchman who finished 37th but in the same time as the day's winner, Pol Verschuere of Belgium.

It is only the second time since the race began in 1903 that Holland has succeeded, and Zoetemelk, who has finished second five times, understandably wept for joy as his team-mate, Gerrie Kentemann, raised his arm in victory after crossing the line.

TI-Raleigh, who secured extra help from Creda this season, have been trying to win this event since they formed the team in 1971. Last winter they secured the biggest close-season transfer when they tempted Zoetemelk away from his French Miko team. Zoetemelk only accepted because

Peter Post, Raleigh's Dutch manager, guaranteed him the full support of the squad in a bid to win the Tour. The team could not have been more successful and apart from winning the team race on points and having the best young rider in Johan Van der Velde, they won 11 stages. "They have won too much," laughed Post, adding, "I've given Raleigh too much value for money in one year."

TOUR IS BROUGHT TO A HALT

Geoffrey Nicholson at Fontaine-au-Pire
The Guardian, 8 July 1982

For the first time in its 80-year history the Tour de France has been stopped and a day's stage cancelled as the result of a political demonstration. Yesterday's fifth stage was to have taken the form of a 73-kilometre team time trial from Orchies to Fontaine-au-Pire through the industrial Nord *département*. This is the kind of event in which the 17 ten-man teams set off to ride the course at intervals of six minutes in a pure test against the clock.

When the first team, the mainly Belgian Wickes-Splendor group, reached Denain after 30 kilometres, they found the vans and decorated floats of the publicity caravan, which normally travels an hour ahead of the tour, blocking the way.

It had been stopped by several hundred steelworkers behind a long banner calling upon the prime minister: "Mauroy, remember the Usinor Denain." As the cyclists came to a halt, members of the gendarmerie motorcycle escort turned back to stop the next three oncoming teams beside the silent and broken-windowed Denain steelworks.

As it became clear that racing was over for the day, some riders reacted with disbelief and annoyance, and a few of those already feeling the strain with evident relief. The cause of the demonstration was the previous day's announcement from the Usinor group that it would close the Denain works, already largely run down, at the end of 1984, with the loss of a further 1,141 jobs.

Various pressure groups including industrial unions and farming lobbies have disrupted the tour before. These events have caused little more than a temporary inconvenience, for a normal stage can easily be restarted. But a time trial is particularly vulnerable, since it is impossible to judge the precise time-gaps between the various teams along the road at the moment that the interruption occurs.

AMATEUR SHARE OF TOUR

by Geoffrey Nicholson

The Guardian, 10 July 1982

Félix Lévitan, one of the two directors of the Tour de France, announced yesterday that next year's race will be open to an equal number of amateur and professional riders. Twenty teams of nine men will compete, the professionals riding in trade teams as at present, the amateurs in national or multi-national teams. Britain would be invited to send an amateur team as well as the USSR, Poland, West Germany, Scandinavia, North America and various countries in Central and South America. Lévitan is still negotiating to begin the 1986 Tour in the United States with a time-trial prologue in front of the White House in Washington, and possibly one or two stages in the New York area. Yesterday the 160 riders of the Tour de France were airlifted on their first rest day from the troubled Nord to what they hope will be less angry Brittany, leaving their drivers, mechanics and soigneurs, the press and the publicity caravan, the telex and telephone operators, the escorts and all the vast army of supporters to follow on 500 kilometres by road. These transfers are extremely unpopular with everyone, though most people grudgingly accept their commercial necessity. There was even a hint of dumb protest last Tuesday when, having been lodged in Luxembourg overnight, the riders were slow to come to the start at Beauraing and the stage got off five minutes late.

HOMECOMING IS A TRIUMPH FOR FIGNON

by Charles Burgess

The Guardian, 23 July 1984

A Frenchman took the overall title, a Scotsman was crowned King of the Mountains, a Belgian beat an Irishman by a heartbeat to win the points competition, and another Belgian won the 23rd and final stage of the Tour de France, which ended in front of 300,000 people on the Champs-Élysées yesterday afternoon, with the Arc de Triomphe as its backdrop.

This marathon that began 25 days and 4,000 kilometres ago in the Paris suburbs has thrown up the worthiest of victors, the 23-year-old Parisian Laurent Fignon, last year's winner. His margin of victory, more than 10 minutes up on the four-times champion, Bernard Hinault, is enormous.

Fignon, the Renault leader, proved himself champion, both in the individual time trials and in the Alps. In fact all the 124 cyclists who finished, out of 170 starters, deserve recognition, having survived the straight roads of the north, the sweltering heat of the west, the torture of the Pyrenees

– where it was so hot the roads turned to liquorice – and the murderous climbs among the Alps.

Robert Millar, the 9-stone Glaswegian, won the second most important jersey, the pink polka-dot of King of the Mountains, and finished fourth overall, the highest-ever placing for a Briton. Sean Kelly, the Irish leader of Skil, lost Saturday's time-trial stage by four-hundredths of a second to Fignon, for the Frenchman's fifth stage win. It was close enough for Kelly to suggest that the result was fixed in Fignon's favour for patriotic reasons.

Over the weeks there have been stories of tragedy, notably the horrific crash involving the Italian Carlo Tonin and a spectator on the descent into Morzine. The Italian is in a coma on a life-support system in Annecy hospital.

MAN MOUNTAIN MILLAR

Geoffrey Nicholson
The Observer, 5 August 1984

An unobtrusive Scot from the Gorbals, Robert Millar won the mountain grand prix in the Tour de France. Millar's was a unique, private triumph, and one which earns him a case of champagne as the Observer/Magnum Sporting Achievement of the Month. He finished fourth in the Tour – the highest-ever place for a British rider – and was the first Briton to win the red polka dot jersey as King of the Mountains.

COKE GET THEIR STICKY FINGERS ON THE TOUR

by Geoffrey Nicholson
The Observer, 23 June 1985

At any time during the past half century, if you were picking a symbol for the Tour de France, it would probably have been that Indian-club-shaped bottle in which they sell Perrier – the drink preferred by *sportifs*, the water which sings and dances.

Not that these particular *sportifs* drank Perrier as they cycled along. Too gassy. The water in their feeding bottles – if it was water and not cold tea or diluted fruit juice – was of a non-vocal, less fidgety brand like Contrexville or Vittel.

But always at the finish of the stage there was a green van with a little balcony on the back from which a hefty, grumpy man of advanced years handed out the Perrier. Clustering around, the riders poured it over their heads or on their swollen feet; some even drank it. And those who had to go up on the podium to collect a special jersey or sash for their achievements in front of the TV cameras invariably found a Perrier bottle thrust into their hands. It was part of the commercial scenery of the race.

Not any longer, though. After 52 years Perrier has been ousted by a foreigner. When this year's race sets out from Britanny next weekend, the feeding bottles clipped to the bicycle frames will be bright red and bearing an even more familiar name in white script. And when each winner takes his bouquet, the other hand will be clutching a can of Coca-Cola (though a fine sticky mess he'll get into if he pours it over it over himself). In all it has been calculated that 62,440 litres of Coke will be distributed free over the next three weeks.

The Society of the Tour de France, who control this and a number of other French tours and one-day classics, don't feel they need to make any excuses. They simply say that Perrier's contract ran out, and that negotiations with Coca-Cola have been going on for some years.

But it is also acknowledged that the American TV channel, CBS, will relay four hours of the Tour this summer, and that the sponsors of these programmes will be Coca-Cola.

AMERICANISATION
To French patriots, who regard Perrier – much as we do milk – as a product above and beyond commerce, this latest development is another alarming step towards the Americanisation of the Tour.

It was in 1982, stirred by the popular success of the World Cup in Spain, that Jacques Goddet, the now-retired director of the Tour, floated the idea of a cycling "*mundial*". This would be a quadrennial Tour which would start in the United States and, with frequent airlifts, visit half a dozen countries before finishing in Paris.

Little has been heard of it since (this is the post-Olympic summer when the first *mundial* should have been run). But Coca-Cola's move, as well as the increasing presence of American pros on the Continent, suggests that the idea, or some variation on it, has not yet been abandoned. Of course what would help to clinch it would be an American victory, or even near-miss, when the Tour ends in Paris on 21 July.

In the absence of Laurent Fignon, the bespectacled winner for the past two years but now recovering from a tendon operation, the clear favourite once again is Bernard Hinault. His apparently unstoppable career was also checked by tendonitis, but any doubts about his current form have been laid to rest by his victory in the Tour of Italy. And as a Breton, Hinault will have tumultuous backing in Friday's prologue on the Plumetec circuit.

But third in Italy, and every prospect of taking the lead if his team-mate Hinault, had faltered, was the American Greg LeMond. World champion in 1983, and certainly not lacking in personal ambition, LeMond might well emerge as a less patient understudy in the French Tour.

There are four other English-speaking runners with a genuine chance – the Scot Robert Millar, the Australian Phil Anderson and the two Irishmen Stephen Roche and Sean Kelly – but just because of his connection with Hinault, LeMond remains the darkest horse. His victory wouldn't upset the organisers but would the French public accept it, after years of European domination, as the real thing?

SHERWEN'S CYCLE OF DOMESTIQUE SERVICE

by Charles Burgess
The Guardian, 13 July 1985

There are 158 riders left as the Tour de France enters its final week and the man lying last is Paul Sherwen, the 29-year-old Briton. He is nearly two and a half hours behind the leader, Bernard Hinault, but his position and time matter not a jot to him or his La Redoute team.

For Sherwen is not, and never was riding the Tour to win. That is the responsibility of his team leader, Stephen Roche, currently third, Sherwen's job is to help Roche at all times, sacrifice himself if necessary and not complain. He is a *domestique*, a member of the poor bloody infantry of the Tour, and he is in good company. More than half the riders are already over an hour behind Hinault and will no doubt lose more time before Paris tomorrow week.

We spoke over tea in the garden of a café in Villar de Lans just after Sherwen had finished Thursday's individual time trial. As the last man he had gone first and joked that as he crossed the line he had the best time of the day. He finished 146th.

He explained the job of a *domestique*, one that he has done for nine years in Europe, coming over here the day after he was awarded his degree in paper technology at Manchester University. "What I had to do in the time trial was to get round without getting eliminated and that meant finishing within the allotted time," said Sherwen. "You get a map of the course, work out what the winner will do and then attempt to finish within 25 per cent of his time. It is a waste of energy to try anything else for I have to be fit for the stages when I can help Stephen. Even if I tried as hard as I could, I would only finish 70th or 80th in a time trial so there is no point."

He continued: "I was an amateur when I first came to France and in six months I was the second best in France. I turned pro with a lot of hopes but turned pro for the wrong team and did not have anyone to explain things to me. After three years I realised I was not going to be a star. But there was nothing degrading about it. Everybody has their limitation and it is just something you have to accept. I realised that you can still have your place as a *domestique*. My job with La Redoute is to look after Stephen. Maybe on a day when he is having a bad time I can help him by shielding him from the wind. But when it comes to the crunch I know he is better than me. On the flat stages I help him to stay as near to the front of the *peloton* (the main bunch) as possible, ideally in the first 20. You have always got to keep an eye out for an attack and that can be very difficult when there are 180 riders. Sometimes you can lose sight of people and have to drop back through to see where everybody is. We have a team meeting every day when we work out and discuss who is dangerous to us, about who not to let get away. If there is somebody who gets away and I am in a good position I will attempt to go with the break and stay at the back to try to slow them down. Although sometimes the bunch is getting out of hand and the team manager will drive up and tell me to stop altogether. Basically the idea is that the team leader should use as little energy as possible until he needs to. On the Tour, after 50 kilometres and up to 30 to go, you can drop back to the team car for drinks. I would do that and also go back for a spanner if the team leader needs to do any adjustments to his bike on the move.

"I have to make sure he does not lose too much time if he punctures. With up to 15 kilometres to go I would stop with him and quickly change his punctured wheel for mine but any closer to the finish would give him my bike, which is almost the same size as his, and then drop back to the team car to get another. With a race this size sometimes the bunch is spread out in a line over two minutes long and Stephen could not afford to wait that long." He added, "On the flat stages when there are bunch sprints my job is to lead Stephen out for the final push. You try to make sure you are on the outside and can leave a gap for him to get through on my slipstream. That is the theory at least."

By his own admission Sherwen is not a man for the mountains, but neither are many of his rival *domestiques*. They form what they call the *autobus*, an alliance that allows them all to ride together to get up the hill in the allotted time and work another day. Sherwen said: "You still have to ride pretty hard but everybody looks after everybody else, lends each other their water bottles to make sure they all finish."

Sherwen survives on this Tour because the judges rewarded his courage for continuing after an accident earlier in the week, even though he finished out of the allotted time. "When I fell off the other day I was out of my mind for a long time. I could hardly pedal and there were times when I could have walked faster. But I said to myself 'you can't get off now, not now.' It would have been a terrible way to end my time on the Tour. I am riding the best race in the world and it would be heartbreaking to stop." Even if he is 158th out of 158.

LEMOND: THEY WON'T LET ME WIN

by Charles Burgess

The Guardian, 17 July 1985

Greg LeMond, the American lying second to his team leader Bernard Hinault in the Tour de France, last night accused his La Vie Claire team manager of not giving him the chance to win the race himself.

The 17th stage, from Toulouse to the clouded ski-station of Luz Ardiden, included the highest climb of the tour and on the final ascent a chink appeared for the first time in Hinault's armour. The man to gain most was LeMond, who picked up over a minute from the Frenchman to move within two and a half minutes overall.

But then there were heated words between LeMond and manager Paul Koechli, who harangued the American for attacking on the way up the 2,114-metre high Tourma-let when he knew his leader was struggling. LeMond angrily pushed away French TV reporters but told the American CBS men that it was obvious they didn't want him to win the Tour. LeMond is paying the price for being the first lieutenant to the French hero who is going for a record-equalling fifth victory.

It was obvious to all the top riders as they wound their way up the 14 kilometres of switchbacks on the Tourmalet that Hinault, who has black eyes after his crash on Saturday, was not at his best.

Two kilometres below the village of La Monge, LeMond, the Irishman Stephen Roche, who is in third place, and two acknowledged climbers, Spain's Pedro Delgado and the Colombian Fabio Parra, pulled away from Hinault's group.

The top of the mountain was shrouded in cloud, and visibility was down to about 100 metres. Roche and LeMond came over the top one and a half minutes clear of Hinault and Roche confirmed later that the American was looking strong and doing his fair share of attacking. After a hair-raising descent back into daylight, Delgado went out on his own and was quickly followed by the Colombian Luis Herrer, wearer of the King of the Mountains jersey. Behind them, the real race was going on with LeMond, Roche and couple of other riders keeping up pace. Hinault was further back in a group including most of his main rivals and as they climbed back into the clouds, the Tour leader was dropped.

INDOMITABLE HINAULT JOINS ALL-TIME GREATS

by Charles Burgess

The Guardian, 22 July 1985

Bernard Hinault was duly acclaimed the winner of the Tour de France for a record-equalling fifth time as the crowds thronging the Champs-Élysées in Paris cheered him home yesterday afternoon. One of the great cyclists of all time, he thus joins the legendary Jacques Anquetil and Eddy Merckx in achieving one of the most extraordinary feats in sport.

He had been true to his word of exactly year ago when, having finished second, he took a full-page advertisement in a French newspaper to announce that "the Badger will be back". It was a victory that everyone had predicted, but not as easy as expected for the 30-year-old Breton.

He survived a crash over a week ago, in which he broke his nose. That injury shook him, and several times on the high passes of the Pyrenees he had looked vulnerable, if only to his teammate, the American Greg LeMond, who finished second. The difference between them, after 23 days and 4,000 kilometres, was just 1min 42sec, a lead cut from six minutes a week ago.

It is easy to analyse where Hinault built his victory. The two minutes he gained when he and the Colombian Luis Herrera formed an alliance to pull themselves clear on the steep climb up to the ski station above Morzine in the Alps were vital, and so were the three individual time trials. In these "races of truth" Hinault was beaten only once and that was on Saturday, near Limoges, where LeMond bettered him by five seconds.

It was the first stage win by an American, not enough to make any difference to anything, but enough to confirm LeMond as the favourite for next year, for already the talk is of 1986. Hinault said yesterday, "This probably will be my last victory. Of course, I have one more year as a rider – I will retire on November 13 1986, because on my 32nd birthday, the next day, I want to celebrate – but the next Tour will ride only to gain victory for a team-mate. If all goes well that will be Greg."

So we must wait for another year to see if an English-speaking rider can break the continental stranglehold in the 73rd edition of La Grande Boucle. LeMond came close enough this year and was convinced he could have won if his team had not stopped him breaking away in the Pyreness on a day when his leader was in trouble. LeMond had to obey orders.

The Californian said: "My stage win convinced me that I can win the Tour one day, because you win it in the time trials. I have many years left. I have helped Bernard to win both the Giro d'Italia (the world's second biggest race) and now the Tour this year, so I hope he will return the favour."

Some say that Hinault's biggest coup was to persuade his La Vie Claire team to hire LeMond – for $300,000 a year and thus nullify his main rival. But there was more to it than that. La Vie Claire had the strongest team overall, able to keep tabs on the rest; and when they were not, Hinault was helped by his rival Herrera, an illegal act that went unpunished.

Hinault, however, always had the psychological edge because for the most part he was riding so strongly and confidently that no one bothered to attack him.

LEMOND MAKES IT ONE FOR THE ENGLISH-SPEAKERS

by Stephen Bierley,
The Guardian, 28 July 1986

Essentially this year's race was about two competitors and two countries. A bit like the Commonwealth Games, really. It was Bernard Hinault, the proud Frenchman, versus Greg LeMond, the haunted American. Yesterday, in the heart of Paris, LeMond was finally declared the winner – the first English-speaking victor of the world's greatest bicycle race, even if he did fall off just before entering the city. The last leg, covering the 158 miles from Cosne, was won by Italy's

Guido Bontempi at the head of a pack of riders. Hinault, who finished 3min 10sec behind LeMond overall, was fourth in yesterday's leg.

It is an all-rounder that wins the Tour, and this time LeMond's younger legs had the edge, even if his mind took one hell of a battering. The 25-year-old Californian was in such a state, during last Tuesday's rest day in the Alps, that in quiet moments he spoke of "unnatural threats" intervening. Was this the Tour de France or *Omen IV*? What strange light was turning behind Hinault's dark glasses?

Well, LeMond made it although many would say it was no thanks to the Frenchman. "I pushed him to his limits," Hinault said in St Etienne, and conceded his challenge was over. LeMond could only reply that if he had known Hinault's intentions from the start, he would have ridden a different race. In the end, however, it made no difference.

BOMB THREAT TO TOUR DE FRANCE

The Guardian, 13 July 1987

Basque terrorists may have been planning to mount an operation against the Tour de France today, when the cyclists are due to complete the 14th stage of the race which begins in Pau and goes through the Pyrenees.

The director of the race, Mr Jacques Goddet, yesterday appealed for reason to people devoted to subversion. A police officer said the Tour had been a target after the arrest of two members of the Basque group Iparretarrak on Saturday. The organisation is prepared to use violence to win autonomy for France's Basque provinces.

ROCHE BECOMES RICH IN 40 SECS

by Stephen Bierley
The Guardian, 27 July 1987

Stephen Roche of Ireland rode into the centre of Paris in the leader's yellow jersey yesterday afternoon to win the Tour de France, the longest and most demanding cycle race in the world.

After three and a half weeks and more than 2,500 miles over plains and mountains, the 27-year-old Dubliner's winning margin was a mere 40 seconds. But those 40 seconds will make him an extremely rich man during the next year.

It was the second-smallest lead since this epic race began in 1903. Roche had made sure of victory in Dijon on Saturday, when he wiped out the 21-second advantage of his only real rival, Pedro Delgado of Spain.

Mr Charles Haughey, the Irish Prime Minister, was in the Champs-Élysées with his French opposite number, Mr

Jacques Chirac, to see the 135 riders pour into the centre of the capital on a sunny, blustery Sunday afternoon. More than 200 had started the race on July 1 in West Berlin.

There are plans to begin the 1989 race in London, but Dublin may now seem more appropriate. Huge celebrations are expected in O'Connell Street today, after Roche and his French wife Lydia, together with their two children, arrive back in Ireland at midday, bound for a civic reception. The Irish tricolour was out in force in Paris, Aer Lingus having coped with a late rush of Irishmen desperate to reach France in time to see Roche's moment of glory.

Roche won the Tour of Italy in June. He was the favourite to win in France, particularly as last year's victor, Greg LeMond of the US, was absent, having been injured in a shooting accident earlier this year. Previously the Irishman's best place was third in 1985. Last year he was injured and finished 48th. He rode the tour for the Italian jeans company, Carrera, but has just signed for the French-registered Fagor, makers of Spanish kitchen equipment.

In a brief comment, Roche called his success unbelievable, adding: "This is a once-in-a-life time experience. Even our prime minister came over to watch it". He said he was looking forward to returning to Dublin.

ANQUETIL: A PRIVATE CHAMPION

Stephen Bierley on the death of a racing legend
The Guardian, 19 November 1987

Jacques Anquetil, one of the legends of European professional cycling, died in France of cancer yesterday after long illness. He was 53.

For anyone brought up in the late 50s and early 60s Anquetil *was* the Tour de France. From 1961 to 1964 he was unbeatable and became one of the immortals of the world's greatest bicycle race, winning it five times. Fellow Frenchman Bernard Hinault and Belgian Eddy Merckx have since equalled Anquetil's record, but he will always be remembered for doing it first. "When I was little he was the champion and my inspiration". said Hinault.

Anquetil, born in Normandy, won the Tour at his first attempt as a 23-year-old in 1957. He was a somewhat aloof, private man, and was not immediately taken to the hearts of the vast numbers of French cycling enthusiasts. But his record earned him their utmost respect.

Like all winners of the Tour, Anquetil was a fine all-round cyclist, although his speciality was the time trial, when a cyclist rides alone against the clock. The Frenchman was capable of annihilating his opponents, building up a huge lead and then blocking for the rest of the race and thwarting the specialist mountain climbers.

He won the Giro d'Italia twice, the first Frenchman to win the leading Italian race, and the Tour of Spain. But his prowess as time trialist is summed up by his capturing of the Prix des Nations nine times in 14 years.

Tommy Simpson, Britain's leading cyclist in the 60s, once said of Anquetil "To be caught by him in a time trial was an experience in itself. For almost an hour before he got past, you could hear the roar of the crowd at the roadside."

In 1965 Anquetil won a special place of affection in the heart of his sternest critics when, after winning the Critérium du Dauphiné and attending the banquet, he hired a private plane to make the 2 am start of the Bordeaux-Paris race, which he duly won. It was a heroic gesture. Two years later Anquetil, who had frequently refused to take part in voluntary drug tests, was banned from the French and World championships. He had gone on record as saying young cyclists starting out on their career should never take stimulants, but added "When you ride 200 days in a year it is practically impossible not to."

To what extent Anquetil used drugs, and whether they ultimately affected his health, may never be known. That he was one of the world's greatest cyclists is undisputed.

NO REPRIEVE FOR PEDRO THE DOPE PEDALLER

by Stephen Bierley
The Guardian, 3 July 1989

There's nowt so queer as folks. Try as it might to adjust itself, this year's Tour de France continued to be dominated yesterday by the extraordinary goings-on of Saturday, when Pedro Delgado seemingly lost his marbles.

It was never going to be a routine prologue, because near the end of the 7.8km course was a nasty little climb. Prologues are usually smooth and flat, offering a little early glory for one of those company of riders whose dearest dream is to see each and every one of the world's inclines bulldozed.

This baby hill, a mere pimple compared to what awaits them in the Pyrenees and Alps, saw the men of strength dominate, all finishing within 30 or so seconds of each other, with Breukink leading the way, followed by a familiar entourage: Fignon, Kelly, LeMond, Bauer, and Mottet.

Delgado should have been there or thereabouts, too. There is a one-minute gap between each of the 198 riders, and as last year's winner he was accorded the honour of starting last.

Cock-ups do occur – riders get snarled up in traffic, stuck in lifts, misread their watches or oversleep – but Delgado had no such excuse. As Sean Kelly, No. 197, rolled away,

Del boy was seen to tootle off in the wrong direction. It was extraordinary.

Explanations bloomed like poppies in a cornfield, explanations provided by people who have usually not been within five miles of the start. Delgado had been seen "drinking coffee in the VIP tent" or "changing a wheel" or "baulked by the Colombians".

None was true. "It was my fault," was Delgado's simple and sheepish answer. He had been signing autographs and missed his turn, handing his rivals a completely unexpected and gratefully received bonus of two minutes and 40 seconds.

"Delgado loses the Tour," pronounced one of France's regional Sunday papers. A touch premature, but nevertheless a ghastly start for the Spaniard, and worse was to follow.

There was never a question of him being disqualified. Time limits are set throughout the race but do not apply to the prologue. A fat chance of Delgado being disqualified anyway, yet he wobbled again in the team time trial, dropping far back at one point before recovering.

CALM BEFORE THE COBBLESTONES

by Stephen Bierley at Spa
The Guardian, 4 July 1989

The Tour de France is a race of startling contrasts. For most of yesterday's third stage the riders threaded their way through rural Luxembourg and Belgium.

But the organisers, never guilty of missing a commercial trick, had arranged a two-lap finish at the Spa-Francorchamps motor racing circuit, where the crowd was huge, the climax strident.

The focus of this week's racing is Thursday's 73km individual time trial from Dinard to Rennes, where Laurent Fignon may close the door completely on Pedro Delgado. Today sees another long stage with a literally rattling good finish: nine sections of those dreaded cobbled cart tracks, the pavé.

Nobody was expecting too many hard knocks yesterday, although the days of "promenade", when the bunch dawdled along, have mostly gone. The pace out of Luxembourg was not startling, and the fastest man was Raul Alcala of Mexico, winner of the white jersey two years ago as the best young rider. He outsprinted Jasper Skibby, Patrick Tolhoek, Thierry Marie and Marc Madiot for his first Tour stage win, and Mexico's too. Da Silva retained the leader's yellow jersey.

Luxembourg, like all good hosts, saved its best until last. Among the wooded hills in the north were towns and villages of perfect charm. A warm sun glinted on the leaded spires of film-set castles, and the café terraces were packed.

Scotland's Robert Millar took the air and the lead for a while, and Sean Kelly earlier helped himself to his share of the lead and some points towards the green jersey.

Fignon and his Super U team were in no mood to drive things along, preferring to conserve energy for Thursday.

Just before the riders entered Spa-Francorchamps a beautiful, throaty roar briefly drowned the interminable pop music as a row of veteran sports cars growled around the circuit. "There goes Delgado," joked a Spanish journalist, more in sorrow than mirth.

Delgado's Reynolds team manager, José Miguel Echavarri, has been explaining that the Spaniard did not eat enough between Sunday's two stages and ran out of energy. Cyclists call it the Bonk, which is altogether different from its yellow-press meaning.

Anyway, bonk he was and bonk he probably still is. If Delgado is not to challenge Fignon, then one looks to Roche, although he hardly exudes confidence at the moment. "I don't stand a chance of winning," the Irishman told French television at the weekend.

As ever, the mountains will sort things out promptly, but for the time being Fignon, who won the Tour in 1983 and 1984, is sitting pretty and thoroughly enjoying the first few days at the expense of Delgado.

So now to those cobblestones, which have not figured in the race for several years. The riders, of course, are delighted to welcome them back – like the Bonk.

DELGADO IS SHOWN THE MOUNTAIN WAY

by Stephen Bierley in Cauterets
The Guardian, 11 July 1989

There is always a special tension on the morning of the Tour's opening mountain stage. On the surface bubbles an edgy cheerfulness, a willingness by the riders to engage in small talk. "But don't ask me any awkward questions," said Canada's Steve Bauer. "I've got too much on my mind."

It was a cool, misty start in Pau. Hawks and buzzards perched motionless by the roadside, miserable as the sprinters. This year's six mountain stages are short, which is some consolation to the flat-earthers. But they threaten to be fast.

The Café de Colombia team were quick to wind up the pace on the initial drag. There followed a thrilling four-and-a-half hours, ending in a first Tour de France stage win for Miguel Indurain.

The 25-year-old Spaniard, a team-mate of Pedro Delgado, had a marvellous spring, winning the Paris–Nice and the Criterium International. He watched France's Robert Forest and Adrie Van Der Poel of Holland take the lead over the opening and demanding Col de Marie Blanque, then caught and overtook them both on the haul to the teetering summit of the Aubisque.

When Indurain entered the village of Cauterets, its narrow streets densely packed and vibrant, there was already a smile of triumph on his face. But the final six kilometres to the ski station, a finish never before used on the Tour, saw him make a couple of anxious glances back.

Another Spaniard, Anselmo Fuerte, was gaining and Delgado had sprung from the tracking bunch, which included Laurent Fignon and Greg LeMond. Indurain hung on while Delgado, now 11th overall, gained 27 seconds on the yellow jersey of LeMond.

Stephen Roche is unlikely to be contesting the yellow jersey this year. He finished the stage more than 14 minutes down on Indurain. "I hit my bad left knee on the handle-bars after eight kilometres when the chain slipped," he said, which seemed, as one Irish journalist remarked, "a feeble excuse". The Dutchman Erik Breukink also had a disastrous stage, down on the winner by 13 minutes.

Fabio Parra of Colombia and Switzerland's Urs Zimmermann will wish to forget yesterday, along with Bauer, but, if the Irish waved goodbye to Roche, they did have Sean Kelly's fourth place to cheer. It is difficult to see anyone prising the green jersey off his back in Kelly's current form and mood.

Fignon took a spill early on but thereafter had everything under control while Charly Mottet survived a dodgy beginning to finish alongside Fignon, Kelly, LeMond and the two Dutchmen Steven Rooks and Gert-Jan Theunisse, the latter looking particularly strong.

Today the climbs are even tougher, including the Tourmalet and another uphill finish to Luchon-Superbagnères. Delgado may decide to attack fiercely here, knowing he will then have three days of relative calm before next Saturday's run from Marseille to Gap and Sunday's individual time trial in the Alps.

Yesterday he had a little dig, a nod and a nudge, towards Fignon and LeMond. Today he will look to slice off a good chunk of the six-minute advantage the pair hold over him. He cannot leave it all until the last week.

EYEWITNESS: PEOPLE'S TOUR BRINGS A MOMENT OF GLORY

by Martin Kettle in Puylaurens
The Guardian, 14 July 1989

The day the Tour de France came to Puylaurens started early for Christian Falco. He had been up all night basting and garnishing a 600-kilogram ox roasting over a wood fire outside the covered market in this tiny hilltop town in south-west France.

Falco, a beefy, bearded master of *cuisine diabolique* from Montpellier, had been roasting his vast joint over an open-air spit since Wednesday, watched by a band of young admirers. Yesterday the scent of roasting meat wafted down the curving avenues of plane trees which would bring the Tour de France into Puylaurens from Toulouse.

It is southern France's great privilege, the national television channel said this week, that it can combine the Tour and the Bicentenaire in one glorious celebration. Yesterday Puylaurens made the most of it.

The Tour was not due until 11.30, but by 9am the route was patrolled by gendarmes, the crash barriers were in place along the Avenue de Toulouse and Pierre Dumondie had taken up his position on a small canvas chair, just at the bend where the riders would leave the town and head east towards Montpellier.

"Almost 20 years since the Tour last came through here," Pierre said. "My father brought me. I don't remember the cyclists, only the crowd. Today I must see the riders."

With two hours to go, workmen begin hanging a banner across the Avenue de Toulouse, marking the first "catch sprint" of the day. Riders can gain extra points by crossing the line first.

At 9.30 the first outrider reaches the town – a Reader's Digest van distributing kitchen whisks. For almost two hours, an ever crazier caravan of advertising vehicles sprints through.

Each slows as it reaches the little square at the top of the town so that free samples and trinkets can be tossed into the crowd. The children shout to each vehicle to stop near them. The old men in their check shirts and berets try to look as if they have seen it all before, but their eyes gleam too.

Vehicles disguised as cigarette lighters, stereo headphones, running shoes and loaves of bread dispense their goodies and disappear to the east, where countless more villages await their moment of glory.

Two hundred years ago the French stretched their hands for bread; today they strain for free plastic bags advertising the World Cycling Championship.

When a gendarme picks up a free audio cassette, everybody whistles and jeers. The gendarme looks bashful, crosses the road, takes off his kepi and presents the cassette to a pretty girl, with a kiss on either cheek. Everyone applauds.

"It's a very sleepy town normally," a bystander says. Puylaurens is a bilingual

Occitan-French town. Most old people do not speak French to each other, and the signposts on the edge of the town are for Pueglauren.

"Five kilometres away," a voice over the Tannoy announces and the advertising vans hastily clear out. Police motorcyclists come through the square at speed. At 11.17 there is cheering down the hill and two emaciated riders come into the square, one in blue and one in red. Number 175 crosses the line first, snatches a swig from his cycle bottle and both ease off.

No one in the crowd knows who they are. Two minutes later, a balding member of the Carreras team arrives, pedalling hard and sweating.

At last the cheers grow deafening. "Here is Fignon! Here is the *peloton*!" The remaining riders enter the square in a sedate and steady swarm. They are a kaleidoscope of multi-coloured jerseys, suntanned thighs, advertising endorsements and whirring wheels. The crowd goes wild.

Only the real connoisseur has time to tell one rider from another. All except one. There in the second row, flaxen hair tied back, is Laurent Fignon, the race leader, wearing the yellow jersey. "*Maillot jaune*. Allez Fignon!" they shout.

In 10 seconds they are gone. The support vehicles, their roofs cluttered with spare bicycles and wheels, follow busily. A large, dark-blue van on which is written *Fin de Course* trundles out of Puylaurens and it is all over.

Within seconds the banners are coming down and the barriers pushed back. Robert Marti, of Puylaurens's Occitan Studies Institute, stands watching. "It's a truly popular event, even today. It's not exclusive and organised like the tennis at Roland Garros. It's in our streets, our countryside and it belongs to the people. And today it was our turn."

LEMOND EARNS THE PLAUDITS IN A DRAMATIC FINAL STAGE – AN ASTONISHING END TO A FASTEST EVER TIME TRIAL

by Stephen Bierley

The Guardian, 24 July 1989

The man on the Champs-Élysées, a Pekinese dog at his feet, dozed for much of an extremely hot morning, waking when his wife unpacked a light lunch of salad, bread and a little red wine. By the time Greg LeMond swept past in the late afternoon for the most remarkable victory the Tour de France has known, man and dog were asleep.

Not everybody is hopelessly in love with this ballad of a race. But nobody who saw LeMond's incredible eight-second win yesterday will forget it. Cycling nerves have never been so jangled. Few had given him a prayer when the race started more than three weeks ago. Now here he was in the winner's yellow jersey again, the coveted jersey he took for the first time in 1986, the last time he rode the race.

It was a quite extraordinary climax to a quite extraordinary 76th Tour. When Jan Janssen of Holland won the *maillot jaune* from Belgium's Herman Van Springel in 1968 in the final time-trial stage, he was largely expected to. Perhaps not even LeMond himself dared dream of such a finish yesterday.

The Californian quite simply rode the stage of his life. "I knew I had to do something very special." He did, riding the fastest Tour time trial ever at nearly 34mph. In his three previous Tours he had never finished lower than third, but few believed, after his shooting accident of 1987 and later injuries, he would get back to the top so quickly or so dramatically. He still has lead pellets in his back, causing him no end of trouble at airport check-ins.

Fignon had never beaten the Californian in a Tour time trial, but that statistic, important as it now appears, seemed to count for less than nothing yesterday morning. Surely Fignon, twice winner of the Tour in 1983 and '84, would not lose this one, at least not by more than 50 seconds. But he did, and the cheers and smiles in Paris were huge.

The 28-year-old Fignon, with his middle-class background and prickly temperament, is no hero of the French. "He rides with his head, not his heart," is the popular response. On this occasion neither head nor body was able to cope. LeMond, crouched over his triathlon-type handlebars, was a praying mantis in search of the Fignon fly.

There were gasps along the Champs-Élysées when it was learned that LeMond, riding one ahead of Fignon, was 21 seconds up at 11.5 kilometres. But still "the wise" curled their lips and shook their heads.

At 14km the Californian was 24 seconds ahead, at 18km the lead had stretched to 29. Fignon was not riding badly, but LeMond was flying.

Excitement, coupled with an acute sense of disbe-lief, vibrated through The crowd. LeMond, all rhythm and complete, detached determination, powered on, his wheels never twitching or deviating. Fignon, knowing the race was slipping away, seemed lumpy and ragged by comparison. His yellow jersey was rapidly losing its golden glow.

"As I came over the line I heard the announcer say Fignon had 20 seconds to win the Tour," said LeMond. "I saw him coming and thought the worse thing that could happen was that I lost the Tour by one second."

If this climax was unbearably dramatic, the start of the Tour in Luxembourg had been unbelievably bizarre. Pedro Delgado, last year's winner, for some inexplicable reason missed his start and lost 2min 40sec. The next day he rode terribly in the team time trial and was suddenly more than seven minutes down on Fignon, always reckoned to be his main rival this year.

It was incredible, almost as if Delgado had been psyched out of the race. In the Pyrenees he chopped the deficit to less than three minutes, but the effort proved too much and he had little left for the Alps.

By now LeMond, who had won the time trial from Dinard to Rennes, taking the yellow jersey in the process, was Fignon's main threat, and with the Frenchman struggling in the mountain time trial to Orcières Merlette, where LeMond re-gained the *maillot jaune*, the chances of the American winning suddenly hardened.

Fignon then turned LeMond's 53-second lead into a 26-second deficit. It was magnificent and courageous riding, worthy, or so it seemed, of a winner. He attacked again on the uphill road to Villard-de-Lans, riding alone for 23km to extend his lead to 50 seconds. The race, it seemed, was over. The action subsided, the status quo was preserved, and all waited for Fignon to claim his third Tour win. It was not to be.

Sean Kelly, still a formidable rider, won the green points jersey for a record fourth time, along with the red catch-sprints jersey. He was always there or thereabouts, although he has not won a stage since 1982.

Robert Millar's moment of glory came in the Pyrenees when he won the stage from Cauterets to Luchon-Superbagnères. In the King of the Mountains class the Scotsman finished fourth.

But the Tour is not, thank goodness, only about results, however remarkable. From the grandness and heroism of the mountains to the crass stupidity of tiny children being allowed to hurl themselves in front of speeding cars to grab plastic bags full of nothing, all human life abounds.

CHAPTER SIX
A TOUR DE FORCE

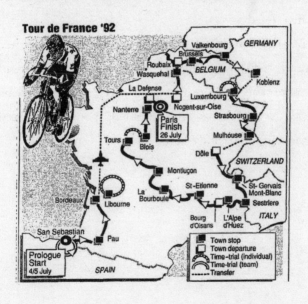

Tour de France '92

FIGNON, SHADED AND JADED, BOWS OUT OF THE TOUR

by Stephen Bierley

The Guardian, 5 July 1990

On a nasty, cold, wet and windy day, the sort thoroughly disliked by professional, amateur and weekend cyclists alike, Laurent Fignon, twice winner of the Tour de France, stepped off his bike, jumped into the warmth of his Castorama-Raleigh team car and abandoned the race.

When the motorbike cameramen closed in at full throttle for a parting shot, Fignon, like an arrested criminal, hastily covered his face with a newspaper. It may or may not have been a copy of *Libération*, but the 29-year-old Frenchman, who took the fabled yellow jersey in 1983 and '84, had indeed freed himself of the Tour. Or, as some later argued, the Tour had freed itself of him.

Fignon is not much loved in his own country and this early exit will curl a few more lips. Last month he had a bad fall in the Giro d'Italia, injuring his back, and he began at the Futuroscope last weekend clearly out of form. Obviously he hoped his legs would respond to the challenge. Equally obviously they did not.

He was involved in a minor crash on Monday between Poitiers and Nantes, and on Tuesday lost 44 seconds to Greg LeMond on the stage to Mont St-Michel. He has never been a rider to prolong a race if matters are going poorly; he also abandoned in 1986 and 1988, in the latter year being the victim of a tapeworm.

Indeed, since 1985 Fignon's career has been littered with ill-health and personal problems. The French, perhaps feeling cheated, turned against the bespectacled, pony-tailed Parisian. But then, last June, on a humid day in Florence, he scored a welcome stage victory in the Giro and the tide seemed to have turned.

Suddenly those heady days of 1984, when he had pulverised Bernard Hinault in the Tour de France, appeared to be back. He had good form, good morale and, above all, good health. He was talked of as a Tour de France winner again.

Even when LeMond took the yellow jersey from him in the Alpine time trial, Fignon sprang back superbly to recapture the lead with a marvellously brave and thrilling ride up the tortuous hairpins to the ski resort at l'Alpe d'Huez.

In any other year he would almost certainly have won the Tour there and then. But the cruellest of blows was lurking on the final day. With only a 23.5km time trial remaining, he led LeMond by 40 seconds. Few believed he would lose, not in his own beloved Paris. But he did.

This year he climbed out of the saddle at the first feeding station. There the team cars were parked. Not for him a degrading ride in the *voiture balai*, or broom wagon, which sweeps up riders who have abandoned. His exit was as brief as it was unexpected. A helicopter awaited. It was sad, but had clearly been planned the day before.

Seen in full cry, as last year, Fignon was an exhilarating sight. His loss is the Tour's loss and in particular France's, for it is unlikely that Charly Mottet or Jean-François Bernard will be able to take up the challenge.

Gerrit Solleveld of the Netherlands won yesterday's gruelling 301km stage from Avranches to Rouen, by far the longest of this year's Tour. The grey, inhospitable weather spurred the *peloton* into early, almost frenzied action with seven riders breaking clear.

Perhaps the startling early pace was the final straw for Fignon, and another to abandon yesterday was Italy's Marco Giovanetti, winner of this year's Tour of Spain. His heart was never in it. The *peloton* eventually bunched again, perhaps gathering around to chew over Fignon's remarkable exit.

Solleveld jumped away at 205km on the descent of the Côte de Lisieux to win by 4min 27sec, with Canada's Steve Bauer retaining the yellow jersey and gaining four seconds at a bonus sprint.

Scotland's Robert Millar, who crashed, lost much valuable time and will be glad of today's rest day when the riders transfer to Strasbourg. For Fignon, every day is a rest day now.

CRASH CLOUDS INDURAIN'S SUNNY DAY

by Stephen Bierley

The Guardian, 29 July 1991

It was almost inevitable, after a Tour de France brimming over with incident and accident, that the last stage into Paris would bring its own drama. On the final swirling, swerving sprint to the line on the Champs-Élysées, Djamol Abdoujaparov, his head down, his front wheel weaving erratically, slammed horribly into the barriers.

A huge gasp went up as the Soviet rider, the winner of the green points jersey, going for his third stage win with his usual determination, flew into the air before falling with a sickening clatter, breaking a collarbone and suffering concussion. Jan Schur of Germany and Stefano Zanatta of Italy also went down. The International Cycling Union is currently trying to enforce the wearing of hard hats but most Tour riders have ignored the ruling. Perhaps this accident will change everybody's minds.

Without a doubt this final crash detracted from the celebrations of the winner, Spain's Miguel Indurain. Even on Saturday, when he effectively won this 78th Tour, he found himself upstaged. With his yellow jersey still sticking to his body with sweat, he sat quietly in a corner after winning the final time trial in Mâcon. In the centre of the room Greg LeMond, showered and changed, held court. "Next year I think I will start favourite for the Tour," the American said. He paused, casting a quick glance in the direction of the Spaniard. "Well, me and Miguel."

Indurain, who as a youngster had no cycling heroes, no cycling posters on the bedroom wall, and apparently no burning ambition, duly made it to the top of the podium yesterday, although as he smiled and waved to the Parisian crowd almost everybody's attention was focused on Abdoujaparov.

In the final time trial through the vineyards of south Burgundy, Indurain had underlined his domination of this year's race with a thoroughly stylish and impressive win. Here was the servant turned master, the team man turned leader.

Yet afterwards it was LeMond who everybody wanted to talk to and Indurain was content to wait. The French, who worry terribly about protocol, hopped about from one foot to the other as the *maillot jaune* was temporarily ignored. They need not have worried. Indurain is accustomed to waiting. For years he has been Pedro Delgado's faithful lieutenant in, first, the Reynolds and then the Banesto teams.

Not a *domestique* exactly but what the French call a *domestique de luxe*. In other words, he was expected to help Delgado on most occasions, but was also allowed, indeed encouraged, to win races of his own.

It was only this year that Indurain began to learn French, the language of the *peloton*, and he has continued to hold his press conferences in Spanish only. This will change as, presumably, will his relationship with Delgado. But for the moment the Banesto team remains one happy family.

By tradition, nobody attacks the yellow jersey on the final day. There was much clowning about on the road from Melun to Paris, with everybody demob happy.

Unaccountably, LeMond took it into his head to break away just before Paris, forcing the Banesto team to work rather harder than they might have wished. LeMond's decision was variously described as panache or sheer bad taste.

PASS NOTES: NO 188: TOUR DE FRANCE

The Guardian, 2 July 1993

Age: 90 on July 3, 1993. But some birthdays have been missed due to interruption by two world wars.

Appearance: Gruelling three-week cycle race for weather-beaten walnuts of men with exaggerated thigh muscles in Lycra shorts and multi-coloured jerseys.

In reality: A way of making lots and lots of money.

What do you mean by lots of money? The Société du Tour de France, the company which organises the race, has an annual income of £13 million.

Combien? Yes, £13 million. £7 million is generated through sponsorship by companies such as Credit Lyonnais, Fiat and Coca-Cola. £2.5 million comes from television rights, £1.5 million is paid by towns and villages wanting the honour of hosting a stage start and/or finish. Also, £35,000 in entrance fees is paid by each of the 22 teams in the race. The rest presumably comes from interest.

But the race wasn't always about product placement? Uhmmm … well, yes it was. Founder Henri Desgrange decided to organise a bicycle race around France in order to publicise his sports paper *L'Auto*.

Why does the race leader wear a yellow jersey? Back to advertising I'm afraid. People complained that they couldn't tell who was leading the race, so Desgrange decided that the leader should wear yellow, which just happened to be the colour of the paper *L'Auto* was printed on.

Essential terms: *Peloton* – the chasing bunch, who may ride in echelon, or cross-formation; *domestiques* – the workhorses who support the team's star riders; *voiturebalai* – broom waggon, sweeping up victims of *le fringale* (hunger-weakness, aka the bonk) and *chutes* (crashes).

Anything different about this year's route? Yes, it's going around France. Last year, the race visited seven European countries: Spain, Belgium, Holland, Germany, Luxembourg, Italy and … oh yes, France.

What do the French think? Happy that the race has returned to its original routes, although unhappy that a French rider has not won the race since Bernard Hinault in 1985. But it has not quite reached the desperate state of British tennis players at Wimbledon.

What else upsets the French? Channel 4's commentary team mispronouncing French words.

And something else they might regard with chagrin? The Tour might come to Britain next year. But only if the Channel Tunnel's ready, so there's hope yet.

What is a Frenchman's favourite Tour joke? Did you hear about the Belgian who won the Tour de France? He did a lap of honour.

Not to be confused with? La Tour Eiffel, Frances de la Tour, La Tour Montparnasse.

Least likely to say: *Prêtez-moi votre pompe.*

TIME FOR THE INDURAIN SHOW

by Stephen Bierley in Verdun
The Guardian, 12 July 1993

The first week of this 80th Tour de France, except for the prologue and the team time trial, has seen the potential winners – Miguel Indurain, Claudio Chiappucci and Gianni Bugno – safe in the anonymity of the *peloton*. Today they must emerge and expose themselves, one by one, to their first serious test.

The Swiss pair of Alex Zülle and Tony Rominger ought to have been among those names, but so far the Tour has gone rather badly for them both. Rominger lost a serious amount of time during the team time trial last week, and towards the close of yesterday's stage from Chalons-sur-Marne to Verdun, Zülle, no stranger to crashes, came a horrible cropper.

Yesterday's stage appeared to be heading towards a sprint finish, with the bunch steadily closing down the lone attack of France's Pascal Lance. Then Chiappucci suddenly attacked on the final hill and the pace increased violently. Poor Zülle was brought down by a camera-wielding spectator whose jacket became lodged in his wheel.

One Lance disappeared, but another spearheaded the final attack to win. Lance Armstrong, a 21-year-old prodigy from Dallas, Texas, has long been touted as Greg LeMond's successor. After his first Tour stage win yesterday Armstrong was asked where he placed this step, compared with his namesake's first step on the moon. "Mars," replied Armstrong modestly.

LeMond was 24 when he won his first Tour stage, the individual time trial at Lac Vassivière in 1985, the year he was second overall. Another lakeside time trial beckons today, and how Armstrong would love to win it. But he will not. "It's not my strong suit – yet."

Last year in Luxembourg, Indurain simply pulverised his rivals during the opening individual time trial. LeMond, absent this year because of illness and lack of form, could barely believe the Spaniard's dominance that year, and afterwards shook his head in bewilderment. In 1991 LeMond, whose outstanding riding against the clock was a feature of his three Tour de France victories, lost a mere eight seconds to Indurain over 46 miles. Last year, on a slightly shorter course, Indurain beat the American by more than four minutes. The improvement in Indurain's time trialing was startling. He has always been good; now he looks invincible.

INDOMITABLE INDURAIN COMPLETES A HAT-TRICK

by Stephen Bierley in Paris
The Guardian, 26 July 1993

Miguel Indurain, who duly paraded in yellow to his third successive Tour de France victory yesterday afternoon on the Champs-Élysées, is not a gregarious man. Indeed, there are times when he displays all the secretiveness of a truffle-hunter.

It is a common sight, on the morning of a stage, to see him riding quietly to the start alone. Often it is only the *maillot jaune* that marks him out, causing a sudden buzz in the crowd and cries of "Allez Miguel" to which he seldom responds.

In the evenings he eats with his Banesto team-mates, although often he leaves the table without his chair being heard to shift. Ask his fellow Spanish riders what he does when he is not on his bike and they reply, with a grin: "He sleeps."

So there was a certain inevitability, given his phlegmatic temperament, about his reply on Saturday when asked if he could now go on to equal the record of winning five Tours that is shared by the two Frenchmen Jacques Anquetil and Bernard Hinault, together with Belgium's Eddy Merckx. Indurain replied he would "take it one step at a time".

Nevertheless it had come as a shock when the Spaniard lost the final individual time trial on Saturday, exposing what many would like to believe are the first intimations of future vulnerability. He offered no excuses but gave the impression, at least during the opening few miles, that the usual zip was missing. It is not easy to tell, for he uses a huge gear and never appears to be pedalling fast.

Tony Rominger, by contrast, always looked to be hurtling along even though the final gap was a mere 42sec. The 32-year-old Swiss had a fine Tour, finishing stronger than Indurain. Besides winning the final time trial he took both stages in the Alps and was second in two of the three Pyrenean finishes. With a little more luck he might, just might, have won the *maillot jaune* instead of the King of the Mountains jersey; that, at least, was the considered view of many.

But, as Greg LeMond once said: "Luck is not part of the Tour de France." After all is said and done, Indurain won by almost five minutes, a larger margin than his two previous wins over the Italians Gianni Bugno and Claudio Chiappucci. Such was his all-pervading dominance, and so badly did all his main rivals bar Rominger crack on the opening Alpine stage from Villard-de-Lans to Serre-Chevalier, that this 80th Tour de France was a little short on raw excitement.

A few years ago the organisers took deliberate steps to "internationalise" the Tour and sell it throughout the world. They must be pleased. This year riders from 11 different countries won stages, including the first Pole in Zenon Jaskula.

But where were the French? Nowhere. Only once, in 1926, the year Monet died, has France never won a stage; this year they managed only one, Pascal Lino's in Perpignan, and their highest rider overall was Jean-Philippe Dojwa in 15th, a new low since 1947.

The Dutch were also short on success and the Belgians remain in the post-Merckx shadow despite a couple of stage wins and having Wilfried Nelissen and Johan Museeuw in yellow for five days.

The balance of power has swung towards Italy and Spain, although Italy has not had a Tour de France winner since Felice Gimondi in 1965 and Bugno, the great hope of recent years, continues to disappoint. A third successive victory in next month's world championships would now have a hollow ring.

Rominger's age is against him but he will be hoping to emulate Joop Zoetemelk, who was 33 when he won in 1980. Many will hope that his fellow Swiss Alex Zülle continues to develop; he finished 41st, more than an hour back, and rather like Bugno appears to suffer as much in the head as the body.

Two years ago Djamol Abdoujaparov, then riding for the Soviet Union, took the green points jersey despite a spectacular crash on the Champs-Élysées. The *maillot vert* was his again yesterday, when he managed to stay in non-flying mode to win the final stage, his third of this Tour and his fifth in all.

Next year, for the first time since 1974, southern England hosts the Tour for a couple of stages. Perhaps by then the BBC will have done its homework and Bob Wilson will not, as he did in an interview this time round, refer to Stephen Roche as "Sean" throughout.

HARD LUC AS BOARDMAN PULLS ON THE YELLOWS

by William Fotheringham

The Observer, 3 July 1994

French television kept repeating the image as if they could not believe it. On the left of Boulevard de la Liberté, finishing straight of the Tour de France prologue in Lille, a floundering Luc Leblanc, leader of the Festina team. On the right, sweeping past with the power and majesty of one of the high-speed trains which will flit in and out of the new TGV station, Chris Boardman, about to become the first Briton to wear the yellow jersey of the Tour de France for 32 years by winning the prologue time trial.

Last year, one British writer described "the Indurain inhalation", the spontaneous uptake of breath when triple Tour winner Miguel Indurain smashed the opposition in a time trial. This year it was replaced by the Boardman bellow.

Boardman's victory had been widely predicted, with the proviso that he had not raced against Indurain or this year's other big favourite, Tony Rominger, when either was on song. What defied belief was the margin of his victory. Indurain was 15 seconds behind in this 7.2 km sprint, Rominger 19 and the rest nowhere.

"Pancake-flat with corners you could take with your eyes closed," was Boardman's verdict on the L-shaped out-and-home circuit along the tree-lined boulevards between the high-eaved Flandrian palaces of old Lille and the hi-tech office blocks of EuraLille, the city's brash new business centre.

Pancake-flat and a mere eight minutes' effort, maybe, but the prologue is still demanding. Thierry Marie of France, prologue winner in 1986, 1990 and 1991, has said: "You just have to empty your head and keep telling yourself: Go for it!" Yesterday, he finished 30 seconds behind, exhausted.

Boardman, for years a time-trial specialist on the British circuit before transferring his talents this year to the Continent, is more methodical: "It takes a lot of bottle not to go flat out all the way. You have to go flat out up to full speed and then relax. It feels as if you're backing off, but you're holding the speed. If you get it right, you blow just as you hit the line."

The prologue always comes as a relief to the riders and race entourage. After the progressive build-up of the preceding weeks and the frenetic nothingness of meetings, medical tests and press conferences, the show is finally on the road.

Today Boardman will start the road stage to Armentières in the yellow jersey, a worthy successor to Tommy Simpson, who held the lead for one day in 1962. Whether he can stay in yellow until the race visits England on Wednesday will depend on two things: how the time bonuses awarded at the stage finishes are shared out, and how his GAN team fare in Tuesday's team time trial to the mouth of Eurotunnel. Whatever happens, he could hardly have "arrived" in more dramatic style.

BOARDMAN ESCAPES POLICE PILE-UP

by William Fotheringham
The Guardian, 4 July 1994

It is an unwritten rule of the Tour de France *peloton* that riders with serious pretensions for the yellow jersey do not get involved in the 40mph *mêlée* of men and machines which traditionally ends a flat stage. These are too risky for all but the fastest sprinters with the steeliest nerves.

Careful inspection of the rule book enabled Britain's Chris Boardman to avoid risking his yellow jersey yesterday when the final metres became a bloodied tangle of bent metal and writhing bodies in the worst sprint pile-up the Tour has seen since Djamolidine Abdoujaparov performed a series of somersaults down the Champs-Élysées in 1991.

Ironically Abdoujaparov, who gained notoriety that year with a series of finish-straight scuffles, was in the clear yesterday and stayed that way to take his sixth career stage win.

The stack was caused by a gendarme taking advantage of being on the wrong side of the barriers to photograph the sprint that was led out at a hellish pace by Wilfried Nelissen, the champion of Belgium, who won a stage last year at Vannes.

Unaware of the 189-strong bespoked behemoth bearing down upon him, the gendarme stood a good 18 inches in front of the barriers – his fellows stood well back, aware that to a sprinter 18 inches is sufficient space for a double-decker bus.

With his head right down, aiming to take the shortest route to the line, Nelissen hit him full tilt and brought down a dozen other riders. Worst off was the 1992 points winner Laurent Jalabert, who was right behind the Belgian and bounced into a giant cardboard Coca-Cola can before falling from several feet on to his face.

Boardman crossed the line 29th after an untroubled first day in the yellow jersey, which he took in stupefying fashion in Saturday's 4.5-mile prologue time trial in Lille in which he broke the Tour's speed record for any time-trial stage, with 34.47mph, and beat Miguel Indurain by 15 seconds.

EDITORIAL: THE TOUR HAS ITS FORCE

The Guardian, 6 July 1994

Compared with this summer's continuing – and, since Monday evening, somewhat deflated – attempt to sell football to the Americans, today's arrival of the Tour de France in England is only a small step in the globalisation of sport.

But there can be little doubt that both are part of the same process. Sport may be the quintessence of nationalism on many occasions, but it is also one of the most effective means yet devised of uniting the global village. If the United States can take to football, and the British fall for the Tour de France, then what price a European cricket championship sometime in the next millennium?

The idea of the Tour de France as anything but a national event still takes a bit of getting used to. As its title implies, it is, well, French. Its founders saw it as a means of uniting the Gallic nation around a genuinely popular event which was not based in Paris – and at the same time creating a nation-wide sale for their newspaper, the ironically titled *L'Auto*. As the Tour evolved, it acquired a heroic image, bred national legends and became the object of fanatical pride and partisan-ship. But the post-war era and the age of commercial, rather than works, teams have combined to force the Tour – like France itself – out on to the European stage. It has become a massive marketing opportunity, as well as a month-long free advert for the French Tourist Office.

For some years, the Tour has crossed boundaries as if they weren't there, which of course now they barely are. In 1992, in what now looks like an ill-judged "salute" to the new Europe, it even managed to visit Spain, Italy, Germany, Luxembourg, Belgium and Holland (where a stage finished at Maastricht) all in one year – as well as managing several days back in the *hexagone* itself.

So the two days which the Tour is spending in this coun-try are very much part of a process of internationalisation. They have their preposterous side, of course. But it is not necessary to be a paid-up Euro-enthusiast to hope that it's a process that will continue. The great thing about the Tour is that, although it is in some ways made for television, it remains a *nonpareil* free popular spectacle. You may see more of the actual race by staying at home. But you will never get the inimitable feel of the Tour unless you choose your place, settle down with your picnic and savour the build-up to the arrival of the riders. They may pass you in a few seconds or, if you have chosen your spot well, over as much as a half-hour. But the feeling of being part of something magnificent is worth all the wait.

SIMPSON? BOARDMAN? NEVER HEARD OF 'EM; FOR THE ROSBIFS IT WAS A NOVELTY, FOR THE FRENCH IT IS AN ANNUAL FESTIVAL.

L'Équipe's Pierre Ballester gives a view from across La Manche
The Guardian, 8 July 1994

In the end, they're not very different from us, these English. They study the professionals' bikes admiringly, they murmur reverently when an unknown cyclist swishes past, they hang around the starting line stuffing themselves – sweet, savoury, hot and cold, all in the same mouthful – they get all excited over a name they recognise, they even talk knowingly about sets of gears they've never even seen before.

On the chalky heights of Dover, with the fortified castle looking down like a great docile tomcat, the Tour was breaking new ground in the face of England's unpredictable weather.

In fact, only the morning was chilly. Some 13,000 subjects of Her Majesty had gathered at the start in a swell of noise from the crowd and the loudspeakers of publicity vehicles;

13,000, of whom one was Steve Solly, vendor of ice creams "created" from the milk of his plump cows.

For Steven, cycling had existed only since the previous day, when he had installed his tricycle near the line. Tommy Simpson, Chris Boardman? No, never heard of them, to be honest. Stephen Roche? 'Fraid not. But if you're talking about Ian Botham, the Platini of cricket, of Steve Davis, virtuoso of the snooker cue, or even golf, which he plays occasionally in his native Hampshire, well …

It was a time of England made in France and vice-versa, of stolid picnics on windy verges, of beer on pub terraces, of polite incomprehension. "But how am I going to get home to feed my dog?" asked an incredulous old lady, prevented by the barriers from getting to the other side of the village. "You've only got a couple of hours to wait," replied an impassive bobby. "Stay where you are and enjoy the show." Delightful, the English sense of humour.

Here and there, in the velvety countryside and the villages hung with bunting, were indeed a few signs saying things like "Buy English Fruit" or "Support the English farmer" – a reminder that digging a tunnel does not create a united Europe. But it was the other things, all the other things, which will be remembered by the competitors and will enthrone the Tour by popular plebiscite.

There were the crowds around the pubs, the school-girls in their blue skirts. There was also John, aged nine, and Jamie, seven, who had been given the day off. "It's super, it's terrific," said an excited Jamie. "But do we have to give back the caps they threw to us?" Super indeed.

Between a well-behaved line of advertising cars and a force of conciliatory police, the Tour beat itself a way through to Brighton and a successful first day. Even the first drops of rain of the Tour failed to spoil the sunshine of popular approval.

But the chef's surprise, the cherry on the cake, was to be produced by one of their own riders, the best-known and the toughest customer. When Chris Boardman took it into his head to get to the front – even if it was only the front of a group pursuing the leaders – the seaside resort of Brighton basked in euphoria. Boardman became Botham and Davis all in one: Boardman showed who he was, that he had it in him, and so what if he was only claiming fourth place: at the finish line he was all jubilation, arms raised, face clenched in the symbolic rictus of the victor.

Translation by Stephen Cook of an article from *L'Équipe*, Thursday July 7, entitled: *L'autre Promenade des Anglais*.

A TOUR DE FORCE AND FATIGUE

William Fotheringham on the heavy toll of stars and domestiques
from the race and the bending of rules to maintain a decent show
The Guardian, 23 July 1994

The first casualty of a Tour de France that has spared neither stars nor *domestiques* came the day before the race began, when the French sprinter Frederic Moncassin tripped on his way on to the stage where the teams were being presented and broke an ankle bone. It was a foretaste of what was to come: a greater proportion of the field retired from this year's race than from any Tour in the last 20 years.

The stars have been forced out in droves since the start three weeks ago in Lille. What a French radio station dramatically called "mass murder" began on the first stage with the carnage when a gendarme tried to take a photograph in the finish straight at Armentières. The two biggest names in the pile-up, Laurent Jalabert and Wilfried Nelissen, were badly hurt and are still recovering from head injuries.

In England a skin infection from an insect bite got rid of Steve Bauer, yellow jersey for 10 days in 1990, and in Brittany the triple-winner Greg LeMond climbed off complaining of persistent fatigue. The Pyrenean 'lergy did for Tony Rominger and Claudio Chiappucci. Gianni Bugno, who never seemed quite sure why he was in the race, bade farewell in Albi and inflamed lungs got too much for Armand de las Cuevas in the Alps.

Then there were the planned withdrawals: Britain's Prologue winner Chris Boardman, the world champion Lance Armstrong and several stage winners: Jean-Paul van Poppel (Boulogne), Nicola Minali (Portsmouth) and Jacky Durand (Cahors).

As of yesterday 70 men – well over a third of the 189 riders who left Lille on July 2 – were at home nursing their wounds, illnesses and exhaustion. At the TVM team, Dag-Otto Lauritzen points out with a wide Norwegian grin that they have "three masseurs, three mechanics, three managers and three riders". Boardman's GAN team are also down to three of their original nine men.

There have been tendon problems, pile-ups and rashes, with stomach trouble the most common complaint. There is not one particularly virulent bug sweeping through the field but a variety of illnesses attacking riders whose immune systems are weakened. "The main reasons are the heat and the speed, which have made the race very stressful," said Gerard Nicolet, one of the Tour doctors. "The riders find it hard to recuperate, they have to drink more and eat differently. They are always on the edge of immunodepression, and one tiny thing can push them over."

However, it might have been worse. On Wednesday, at the Tour's highest ever stage finish, Val Thorens, 68 of the 126 riders finished outside the time set for the stage and faced disqualification. Fortunately for them the organisers decided a field reduced to 58 on the Champs-Élysées tomorrow would not look good and allowed them to remain in the race. The last time they showed such clemency was in 1976.

Life in the "*autobus*", or "*gruppetto*", the sprinters and *domestiques* who ride together through each mountain stage with the sole aim of finishing inside the cut, can be as stressful as it is at the head of affairs. The margin for error is small: one or two of the more experienced riders calculate how much time can be lost on each mountain, and set the speed using the mini-computers most Tour cyclists carry on their handle-bars. One of the "bus drivers", the Italian Guido Bontempi, explained: "You work out what the time of the winner will be, allow an extra five or 10 minutes for error, look at where you all got dropped, and how much time you can lose."

There can be tension if there is disagreement over the speed: such an argument on Mont Ventoux last Monday ended in an impromptu roadside boxing match between the Australian Neil Stephen and the Mexican Raul Alcala. As team-mates tried to separate the pair, Stephen suffered a broken nose and a black eye. "You can't relax if everyone thinks only of themselves," explained Italy's Eros Poli. On Wednesday, however, the tailenders opted for solidarity in the hope – eventually realised – that the organisers could not throw all of them out.

The stages feared most by the regular occupants of the *autobus* are short legs with a mountain finish such as Wednesday's: the cut will always be a short one. What they dread is a high pace up the opening mountain, which will mean they wave goodbye early on to the pure *grimpeurs* and face a longer struggle to finish.

Often agreements are made to prevent hotheads, who frequently tend to be Colombian and Spanish, making the rest suffer. "On Wednesday all the big guys sat at the front of the bunch and blocked the road on the first climb," said England's Sean Yates, who wore the yellow jersey earlier in this Tour.

Behind the "*autobus*" come the stragglers, followed by the dreaded sight of the *voiture balai*, or broom wagon, which "sweeps" up riders who decide to abandon. Georges Laborie, the man wielding the besom, said: "We've had a lot of work this year – too much. It's been pitiful to watch. On the stage to Montpellier there were 12 or 13 riders in the van. They didn't say a word. There was silence."

Riding alone in the mountains with the *voiture balai* for company is one of the most painful experiences for a rider:

the prospect of an end to his suffering is chugging away behind him.

"You try not to think about getting in but sometimes you can't keep the thoughts away," said Italy's Mario Mantovan, a *domestique* in the Carrera team, who struggled for 60 miles in front of the broom wagon on Tuesday's stage to l'Alpe d'Huez. Two days later the temptation proved too much and he climbed into the FIAT van, as so many had before him this year.

A SPOKE IN THE NEWS: THE TOUR DE FRANCE IS HOT, SWEATY AND UPHILL WORK FOR THE JOURNALISTS

Pedro Blasco reports on the time trials and tribulations of the men who pedal the news
The Guardian, 24 July 1994

The cyclists are the heroes of the Tour de France, but behind the images seen daily by millions of viewers lies a media circus that cranks into gear as each stage comes to an end.

Some 4,000 people work on the Tour; around 700 journalists from around the world are there to tell the tale. If life is tough for the riders, it can also take its toll on the journalists. In the past 15 months, four have died covering cycling races: two Spaniards and two Italians.

During the Tour journalists receive information free. But use of the telephone costs an average 40,000 pesetas (about £220). The organisers don't seem to realise that many reporters covering the Tour don't file their stories by telephone.

But the amenities aren't bad. A table, a folding chair, a results service, a Coca-Cola, and the threat of a heart attack when the journalists realise they have a bad connection and can't be heard or the radio report they've just filed on the race is lost in the static.

For the press corps, the working day is hard. Some years ago, they did their interviews and wrote their reports at nine in the morning in the "village", a sort of corral. While the cyclists sipped their coffee, the scribes and photographers quietly got down to work.

But a free bar was erected and now it's full of freeloaders eating breakfast and pocketing the sandwiches. Cyclists and journalists have been expelled: if you want to get Indurain, you have to catch him.

When the starting signal goes off, the journalists jump in their cars and set off for the finishing line. Watching them pass is risky, while to overtake the *peloton* is plain dangerous. If you cause an accident, the organisers can withdraw your press accreditation for anything from one to 21 days.

In the press room, if the morning has gone well, journalists trade interviews. One "Indurain" is worth one "Bugno" and one "Chiappucci". Fine and proud journalist exchange news with reporters from other countries as if they were swapping cigarette cards.

The Tour news for the journalists comes from Radio Tour, which transmits every racing moment, and a computer in the Press Room, often a few kilometres from the finishing line.

When the cyclists reach the finishing line they are received by a *mëlée* of reporters, pens and microphones in hand, trying to get words out of men hardly able to walk. The stage winners or the leader of the Tour climb into a mobile press room where they utter their first words, later to be repeated for the benefit of a larger audience. For many of the journalists present, this is the closest they will get to a cyclist during the whole Tour.

When the day is over, and the reporters have filed their stories, it's off to a hotel that could be anything up to 60 kilometres away. At eight the next morning the alarm clock goes off and off we go. It's time to chase Indurain again. Such fun, the Tour.

Guardian/El Mundo

TRAGEDY STRIKES THE TOUR: OLYMPIC ROAD-RACE CHAMPION DIES AFTER HIGH-SPEED CRASH

by William Fotheringham and Alex Duval Smith

The Guardian, 19 July 1995

Fabio Casartelli was killed yesterday after crashing and hitting his head on a concrete post during the toughest mountain stage in the Tour de France. The 24-year-old Italian Olympic road-race champion was the third rider to die in the race's 92-year history and the first since Britain's Tommy Simpson collapsed from heat exhaustion in 1967.

Inevitably in an event where 189 cyclists share a small stretch of tarmac, accidents are common: the final phase of every flat stage in this year's race has seen a spate of spills, while riders have fallen off in every mountain stage. Usually the result is broken bones in the hand or shoulder as riders attempt to break their fall.

This crash was different. The descent from the Col de Portet d'Aspet to the village of Ger de Boutx is as steep as one in seven in places and the tarmac is badly cambered on the tight hairpins. The route is rimmed by square concrete blocks, designed to prevent vehicles from going over the edge.

Casartelli fell after losing control on a bend and hitting his head on one of these posts. He lay unconscious on the road with blood pouring from his head wounds. His fall brought a number of other riders down, including the Frenchman Dante Rezze, who fell into a ravine and broke a thigh bone, and the German Dirk Baldinger, who suffered a fractured hip bone.

Casartelli was taken unconscious by helicopter to Tarbes with severe head injuries and died 30 minutes after reaching hospital. En route to Tarbes he was treated by Gerard Nicolet, one of the race's doctors. Nicolet said the density of riders on the descent – and by implication Casartelli's inability to manoeuvre – was more to blame than the fact that he was not wearing a protective helmet.

Ironically, it was in the Pyrenees in 1991 that the Union Cycliste Internationale dropped its attempt to impose protective headwear on professional cyclists. Shell helmets were made compulsory at the start of that year, but sit-down protests and a threatened boycott of the major classics forced the UCI to adopt a compromise that was scrapped after riders refused to start the Tour stage that was to take them across the Pyrenees in intense heat.

THE GIANT WHO DOES AS HE LIKES

by Richard Williams

The Guardian, 24 July 1995

As Miguel Indurain passed for the final time he was in 101st position, disappearing down the Champs-Élysées towards the Tuileries, rolling along at the rear of the field on the last lap of a race that began in the rain of Brittany three weeks ago and finished in bright Parisian sunshine yesterday.

Indurain won the Tour de France for the fifth consecutive time yesterday, an unprecedented feat so remarkable that it was worth missing events at St Andrews and Donington Park in order to be present at the celebration.

For no sporting event in the world is harder to win than the Tour, and there is no contemporary sportsman or woman more extraordinary than the giant from Navarre, who can draw eight litres of air into his lungs at a single gulp.

This race was wrapped up days ago, probably at the ski resort of La Plagne, when Indurain stepped on the gas in the mountains and showed that he simply could not be beaten.

"What he did there was exceptional," said Bernard Hinault, another champion. "On this tour Miguel hasn't just surprised me. He has astonished me. He's done exactly as he liked. He didn't panic. He saw everything and dominated everything."

Hinault is one of the three men – Jacques Anquetil and Eddy Merckx are the others – who have also won the Tour five times. But none of them managed five in a row. And in Hinault's view Indurain has already won his sixth – back in 1990, when he obeyed team orders and fell back to protect his leader Pedro Delgado.

Had he attacked, Indurain would in all probability have finished first instead of 10th, commencing his sequence of victories a year earlier than he managed. At this stage no one would cast doubts on his ability to do it again next year.

He is 31 years old and says that he is riding with more confidence and aggression than ever. His maturity enables him to focus his energy and to time his attacks with devastating suddenness, catching his enemies unprepared.

He remains the master of the time trial, imposing that infernal rhythm with an absolute belief in his own capacities, and he is a good enough climber to compare with the specialists. All he lacks is the finish to win a bunch sprint, but then no sprinter has anything like his all-round qualities.

An hour before the race's scheduled arrival in Paris the spectators were already six, seven and eight deep all the way along both sides of the Champs- Élysées, some standing on benches and refuse bins, others perched on the branches of the chestnut trees that line the avenue between the Place de la Concorde and the Rond-Point.

Hundreds of thousands thronged the streets, which had been closed for several blocks in all directions, the cafés were full, the souvenir vendors were doing a brisk trade in caps, pins and T-shirts, martial music blared from the public-address speakers and the trampoline champion of France gave a demonstration to the crowd assembled in the vicinity of the Grand Palais.

As gendarmes cleared the boulevards, the city was transformed into a rural village *en fête*, as long as one could ignore the Drug Store, the McDonald's and the multiplex cinema showing *Batman Forever*.

Outside a pizza restaurant a dozen guitarists and mandolin-players from Cordoba performed a tribute to Indurain by serenading the lunch-time crowd with manly songs of national pride and individual achievement. Or that is how they sounded, anyway. Spanish flags were everywhere, while the only tricolours were the official ones hanging from the lamp standards.

Two years ago, as part of what the organisers called the "mondialisation" of the race, the Tour de France was renamed simply "Le Tour". Since its first edition, in 1903, the race has harboured persistent dreams of taking over the world.

Often it visits other countries – last year England, where more than a million spectators turned out to welcome it; this year Belgium. Sometimes it has even started on foreign soil: Frankfurt in 1980, Basle in 1992.

But now the race is once more called the Tour de France, a belated recognition of the fact that what attracts people to the event is not merely its uniquely gruelling nature or its incomparably rich history but its absolute Frenchness.

The Tour does not need to go out to the world; in Paris on Sunday at the end of each July, the world comes to it. The concluding laps over a circuit around the Jardin des Tuileries and up to the Étoile is not one of the Tour's older traditions.

It was inaugurated only in 1975 but in 20 years it has become one of the great set-pieces of world sport. Yesterday the atmosphere built steadily as the *peloton*, which had been taking it easy on the run from Sainte-Geneviève-des-Bois, neared the city. This provided plenty of time to enjoy the passage of the publicity caravan: the Coca-Cola girls, the parade of vintage motorcycles, the vehicles built to resemble oranges, cellular telephones, slices of Camembert or cans of insecticide. And it allowed a moment of glory to the drivers of the giant articulated technical support trucks, which boomed over the cobbles two abreast, their horns sounding off like ocean liners.

The frisson spreading through the crowd when the cyclists eventually erupted out of the Rue de Rivoli, across the

Place de la Concorde and into the Champs-Élysées through the dust-filled air rivalled the sensation of the Derby leaders rounding Tattenham Corner.

There, with a magnificent sense of theatre, were the Banesto riders, all nine of them, the only complete team left in the race, leading the yellow jersey up the avenue towards the Arc de Triomphe. Whatever happened in the remaining laps, we had been given the opportunity to applaud the hero, which was, after all, why we had come.

VILLAVA SALUTES ITS MIGUELON

by William Fotheringham

The Guardian, 25 July 1995

Back in the days when Miguel Indurain's family were not sure if he should head off to France for four weeks to ride a bike race, his manager would assure Miguelito's peasant-farmer father that his son would be back by the time he was needed for the harvest. Indeed, Indurain abandoned his first two Tours before the race was half done.

But in 1991, when he won his first Tour, Miguelito became Miguelon – Big Mig – and every year since then the harvest has been well and truly in, in every sense, when he has arrived back in his home village of Villava, just outside

Pamplona and no more than 25 miles from the French border. His annual post-Tour victory welcoming party usually brings out the entire town but this year it was estimated half the 15,000 population had gone off to Paris for Sunday's finale.

Yesterday, after being proclaimed "King Miguel of Navarre" in the provincial parliament in Pamplona, he was welcomed home to Villava with church bells and rockets. One of the first things he did was to dedicate another yellow jersey to the town's patron saint, the Virgin of the Rosary.

"For me it has been a tough Tour but also a moving one. I'll try to prepare with all my strength to be right here next year," Indurain declared. It was a far cry from his return in 1985 after he pulled out of his first Tour in the Pyrenees.

Like a robust seedling Indurain has been nurtured over the past decade, his progress as a professional mapped out by the sports doctor Sabino Padilla of Pamplona University and Banesto's current team manager, José Miguel Echavarri.

The Tour's other five-times winners, Jacques Anquetil, Eddy Merckx and Bernard Hinault, all won at their first attempt. By contrast it was in his third Tour that Indurain even reached Paris and his fifth where he earned a stage win.

With this year's campaign over, Indurain says he feels fresher than ever before, and he looks it. The contrast with the two men expected to run him close could not have been greater: Tony Rominger was an exhausted and unhappy eighth and Evgeni Berzin is recovering from a lung infection. Rominger declared last week that anyone aiming to win the Tour will have to devote his entire year to it, to the exclusion of all other races, as Indurain does.

Cycling is now too stressful for riders to spread their efforts over a whole year as Merckx, Hinault and Sean Kelly did. Indurain rode only one of the spring one-day Classics; the only rider to do well in the Classics and the Tour, indeed the only man to race both seriously, was Laurent Jalabert.

Significantly, though, the Frenchman took a five-week break from racing during late April and early May and is convinced he owes his Tour green-jersey points title to that. The traditionalists may throw their hands in the air, but cycling has been dragged into the modern world by a big man from Navarre.

OBITUARY: PIERRE CHANY

by Adam Glasser
The Guardian, 5 July 1996

Pierre Chany, who has died aged 73, covered every major continental cycling race since 1947 and wrote about nothing else. His outstanding books on the Tour de France and the

Classics have become definitive reference works. Had it not been for his fatal bout of pleurisy Chany would now be in the press caravan following his 50th consecutive Tour de France.

We somehow expected him to carry on forever. A book entitled *L'Homme aux 50 Tours de France*, based on several long interviews with him, had just been published in France. Although fate, sadly, has falsified the title, Chany's record of 49 Tours is unlikely ever to be equalled. He seemed to have a constitution of iron and a voice made gruff by smoking too many cigarettes. Last year he was forced to abandon his first race ever – frostbitten fingers during the early spring briefly left him unable to type.

Born in Langeac in the Haute Loire region of France, Chany began his working life as a locksmith while pursuing a good amateur racing career. After active service in the Resistance, he followed his first Tour de France in 1947 as a journalist, a "Tour of Enthusiasm" as he described those early days on the back of a motorbike exposed to the same hazards as the riders – the gruelling heat of the plains, alpine thunderstorms and treacherous untarred mountain passes.

The task of telegraphing his "*papier*" back to Paris was always a test of ingenuity. "With chocolate or a bottle of aperitif, we would persuade the local postmaster to reserve the line for our use," he recounted. But he was also a professional who moved with the times – until his recent illness, you could find Pierre in the "*salle de presse*" after a cycling race, tapping away on a laptop and using the latest technology to file his copy back to the office.

On first meeting him some years ago in Morzine, I was struck by his small, compact stature. I had imagined him to be a giant after reading his reports in the prestigious French sporting daily *L'Équipe*. Whether describing low-life detail or moments of epic grandeur, his writing had a fine quality of observation – he would liken traces of snow on the roadside of the Tour of Flanders to ermine lining a royal path. His gift of relating what he saw in the present to the great mythical heroes of the past was never excessive or sentimental.

One of his most memorable pieces was a portrait of L'Abbé Joseph Massie, the priest of Bastide d'Armagnac, who worshipped cycling and founded the parish "Notre Dame des Cyclistes". Chany describes the good abbé's joy in 1989, when he welcomed celebrities from the Tour de France caravan into his church crammed with a fantastical collection of cycling relics, before setting the riders off on their way with a blessing.

Chany's profound concern for the long-term well-being of his sport saw him fearless in his criticism of its governing bodies. He rounded on the recent tendency to export major races to countries with no culture of cycle racing: "China or

Colombia I can understand … but to stage the World Championships in Japan is like holding a bullfight in Scotland".

Chany was one of those writers who never sought recognition. It came to him quietly of its own accord. Over the years he received a host of literary and journalistic awards. He also created the "Prix Pierre Chany", given each year to the author of the best cycling article in French.

Pierre Chany, writer and cycling journalist, born December 16 1922; died June 18 1996

TOUR ENJOYS TV BOOM

by Mark Redding
The Guardian, 8 July 1996

Couch potatoes worldwide can rest easy: the Tour de France has no intention of going pay-per-view. Approaches have been made from cable television in the United States, sparking fears that future coverage in Europe could go down the pay-per-view route, but the organisers this week promised to remain firmly anchored to the major networks. "We want our exposure to be as wide as possible," said Yann Le Moenner, in charge of international sales for ASO of Paris, the company that oversees the Tour de France. "It is the only event that has so many spectators and we want it to remain free."

In Britain the Tour has become associated with the excellent highlights package shown each evening on Channel 4. The producer Brian Venner cut his teeth on *Grandstand* and that BBC pedigree shows: his VTV company, which supplies the highlights, has taken the industry's independent award for best sports programme for the past three years.

The show's mix of action, features, crashes and tourism pulls in a healthy audience for Channel 4 of 1.5 million. This is on top of the 600,000 or so who watch the unedifying coverage of Eurosport, which is transmitting the event live this year for the first time.

So when "Lights, cameras, action!" is called on Stage 9 of the Tour in Val-d'Isère today, it will not just be Miguel Indurain flying by the seat of his pants. Back in the Channel 4 studios Venner will be rushing around in the two hours between the end of the stage and the programme's transmission, trying to find out who has shot what.

That means pasting together a collage comprising pictures from the main feed, shots from other countries' crews, and film taken from the back of a roving motorbike by his on-the-spot cameraman Glenn Wilkinson.

Venner also has to find a way of dealing with the myriad unexpected disasters that can occur. In 1988 Wilkinson was taken hostage by irate Frenchmen after his driver bent a spectator's bicycle and he was not released until the damage had been paid for.

Then there was the fiasco in 1992, when Wilkinson was looking forward to unwinding after the usual demanding day. "I was lying in my bed in San Sebastian and about two in the morning I heard shouting," he said. "I saw some flickering and looked out the window and our cars went whooooooosh." Channel 4's vans had been torched by Basque separatists.

LEADING TEAM IN TOUR DE FRANCE THROWN OUT OVER DRUGS

by William Fotheringham

The Guardian, 18 July 1998

France's euphoria after the triumph of the World Cup has proved short-lived. The country's greatest sporting institution, the Tour de France, is in crisis following the expulsion of its leading team after the biggest drug scandal to hit the race in its 95-year history.

The Festina Watches team were thrown out last night, nine days after the arrest of team masseur Willy Voet on the Franco-Belgian border. His car contained 400 flasks of the banned drugs erythropoietin, human growth hormone, and anabolic steroids.

Erythropoietin, commonly known as EPO, is a hormone which stimulates the bone marrow to produce red blood cells, thus increasing performance. It is usually taken with aspirin to prevent blood thickening, which can lead to heart attacks.

Human growth hormone assists the body to recover from physical effort.

On Wednesday, the Festina team manager Bruno Roussel and the team doctor, Eric Rijckaert, were arrested and questioned. Yesterday, Roussel's lawyer, Thiboult de Montbriault, issued a statement confirming that riders were supplied with banned drugs. "Roussel has explained the conditions in which riders were provided with doping products, and how this was organised by the team management, the team doctors, the masseurs and the riders. The objective was to maximise the riders' performance under strict medical control to prevent them obtaining drugs for themselves in ways which could seriously affect their health."

Roussel and Rijckaert have been charged with supplying drugs at sporting events.

Festina have not won a stage so far in this year's Tour de France, but they won four stages, and were the best team in the 1997 race, led by France's national hero, Richard Virenque. He finished second and was crowned King of the Mountains for the fourth successive year. They currently hold the number one position in cycling's world computer rankings. Also banned was Laurent Brochard, world elite road racing champion.

Since the seizure, the riders have insisted on their innocence. Yesterday, the Frenchman Pascal Hervé, who was leader in the King of the Mountains competition when he was excluded, protested: "I didn't take erythropoietin. The only products I took were things to help me recover so that my form could be good."

The Tour de France organiser Jean-Marie Leblanc, a former professional cyclist himself, said the riders were being excluded as "a lesson to the Tour de France and cycling which we hope will be a salutary one, and will end the unhealthy atmosphere which has been present on the race".

The long-term effects on the Tour and cycling could be devastating. There has been continual speculation over drug taking in this most demanding of endurance sports. The scandal calls into question the sport's ability to govern itself.

DOPED RIDERS ON THE STORM

The drugs scandal will haunt France long after the teams cross the line today, reports Arnold Kemp in Paris

The Observer, 2 August, 1998

It was 9.30pm when the police came for Ródolfo Massi, entering his hotel by a back door. They searched his room and found corticoids in a case. They gave him time to shower and eat before taking him to the police station. Then they drove him north from Chambery in Savoy to Lille and to the lair of Judge Patrick Keil who, with a little help from his friends, has brought the Tour de France close to oblivion.

On Tuesday Massi, who rides for Casino, had won the right to wear the polka-dot jersey as King of the Mountains. Now the Italian star had set another record: he became the first rider in the 95-year history of the tour to be arrested on suspicion of criminal behaviour.

Massi was placed under judicial examination and locked up. On Friday, claiming he had been stitched up by a rival settling old scores, he was released on bail. He said the corticoids, in the form of nasal sprays, were for colds.

But the discovery of the drugs, which police said came from Italy, Greece and Holland, changed the direction of the inquiry. Until then riders had been considered as simple victims of doping imposed by team managers, coaches and commercial pressures, but Massi's examination meant their complicity was now in the firing line.

The next day, the tour crossed into Switzerland. Now on neutral territory the five men in the team sponsored by the Dutch transport insurance group TVM made good their escape from French justice. On Tuesday evening they had been taken from their hotel at Albertville; their blood, urine and hair had been tested for drugs. They were told on Thursday to report to the authorities in Rheims the following Monday. They left for the Netherlands.

They became the seventh team to leave the race. A number of star riders have also quit. The cyclists who finish the tour on the Champs-Élysées today will be a tattered fragment of the army that set out from Dublin on July 11. Of the 21 teams, 14 remain and of the 189 riders, only 96. Back along the grinding route are broken dreams and shattered reputations.

The race that occupies an honoured place in modern French mythology, a byword for courage and endurance, a bonding festival of high summer, has been exposed as a sham founded on hypocrisy and criminal behaviour.

The doctors who run the teams have emerged as sinister "sorcerer's apprentices" taking ever greater risks with the riders' health. The sponsors, on whose largesse the race depends and who are rewarded by intensive TV coverage, have been left with their names covered in mud.

The judicial authorities were accused of treating the riders "like animals". The police denied allegations that they conducted internal searches of TVM players being tested at a local hospital. But the police treatment of riders fed anger and even panic in the *peloton* (pack). On Wednesday the race was twice stopped and, in a go-slow, riders removed their numbers to invalidate the stage, finishing it in mutinous anonymity hours late. Spectators vented their anger both at the officials, at one point "mooning them", and at the riders, whistling and booing them.

Yet Keil and his fellow examining judge, Odile Madrole in Rheims, have been prepared to risk one of the biggest scandals in the history of sport to confront what Sports Minister Marie-George Buffet last week denounced as "a vast traffic in dope products that puts human lives in danger".

The story of the putsch against the Tour begins last year but the authorities deliberately delayed decisive action until the race started – only when it was in France could they get their hands on the evidence they needed.

It was last year that Buffet declared war on doping in sport and initiated new laws against it. They are still under consideration by the French parliament but existing statutes are prohibitive enough. At the start of this year regional conferences were held to raise the authorities' awareness of the campaign.

In March, customs officers in Rheims intercepted a vehicle belonging to the TMV team and found 104 doses of erythropoetin, or EPO, which enhances performance by promoting red blood cells.

The drug, which can have dangerous side-effects, is believed to have been in use on the tour for about six years. At the time no action was taken by the prosecuting authorities in Rheims.

On July 8, near the French border, Belgian customs officers stopped a car driven by the Belgian Willy Voet, trainer of the team sponsored by the Andorran-based watchmakers Festina. It had taken an odd route after leaving the Festina HQ, near Lyons, heading first into Switzerland and then Germany before turning west to head for Dublin and the Irish "prelude" to the tour.

The car had been spotted several days earlier at the French-Swiss border, and aroused further suspicion when it was observed sticking to quiet backroads. It contained 400 doses of drug products, including 250 of EPO and 100 of anabolic steroids.

Two days later the public prosecutor in Lille ordered Judge Keil to begin an inquiry, under the French process of investigative justice which must precede any criminal trial. As a result of testimony from Voet and from other Festina officials and riders, the team doctor, Eric Rijckaert, a Belgian, was detained. He remains in custody.

Three damning pieces of evidence emerged. Festina coach Bruno Roussel admitted that riders were provided with drug products "under strict medical conditions". Then Belgian police gave the French authorities computer records seized from Rijckaert in an earlier operation. These apparently detailed the medication given to Festina riders.

Faced with this evidence, five of the nine Festina riders admitted that the team had a "black bank" or slush fund to which they contributed their bonuses to buy drugs – estimated to be at least £10,000 per year per rider and perhaps much more.

On July 17, the Tour organisers banned Festina, saying it had departed from required ethical standards. But the evidence being gathered by police on the warrants issued by Keil was now implicating other teams and riders. Massi, who used to ride for Festina, was identified by an old team-mate as being the team's principal provider of drugs.

On July, 23 customs in Rheims reopened its investigation, dormant since March, into TVM. As in Britain, customs officers have wider powers than police, who must act on magistrates' warrants. A customs raid on the Dutch team's hotel at Tarascon-sur-Ariège found cases of performance-enhancing drugs, and others to mask them. Coach Cees Priem and team doctor Andrew Mikhailov were taken to Rheims, where Judge Madrole opened a parallel judicial inquiry and issued warrants.

The consequence was the evening raid on the TVM hotel last Tuesday, by about 30 officers, which almost brought the tour to a halt the next day. A policeman who took part in the Albertville raid said he was stunned by the enormity of what they were doing. "We were just about as upset as they were," he said. "The Tour is sacred for us, too. It's almost iconoclastic to touch it."

By the end of the week five other teams had quit. Once, the team of the world number one Laurent Jalabert, returned to Spain in high outrage, denouncing the French judicial system. "Worse than Chile under Pinochet," said a Spanish newspaper. Drugs had been found in one of Once's trucks and its doctor was placed under examination and released on bail on Friday.

Some commentators have seen the vents as a sign that the old "complicity" in French society is over. They compare it to the decision to bring to trial former Socialist Prime Minister Laurent Fabius and two of his Cabinet Ministers on charges arising from the deaths of patient who received transfusions of blood carrying the Aids virus in 1985.

Others are less certain about casting a lurid light on a practice that has long been commonplace in the Tour and has been tacitly tolerated by the public. Bernard Kouchner, the Secretary of State for Health, whose father was a Tour doctor, said: "We're all accomplices in this gigantic hypocrisy because everyone knew that doping reigned in the Tour."

Perhaps what has changed attitudes more than anything else is the sense that team doctors are now taking unacceptable risks and applying programmes which administer drugs every day from October, with ever-increasing doses of EPO, testosterone and anabolic steroids.

Buffet said the traffic in doping implied hierarchies of providers, manufacturers and secret funds. "In the search for truth, we must go right to the end," she said.

After the finish today, the International Union of Cyclists begins a daunting task of damage limitation. A German member of the Festina team, speaking just after giving evidence to police, said: "The union will have to suspend more than 100 riders after the Tour."

Since fewer than 100 will cross the line, that implies a total wipe-out of professional cycling. A commentator remarked that for many French people, the Tour is a rite of passage, like losing their virginity. The race is part of a collectively remembered idyll of adolescent summers. But virginity, once lost, is gone forever, and innocence too.

VIRENQUE AT THE END OF THE ROAD: THE WHEELS HAVE COME OFF FOR FRANCE'S HERO

by William Fotheringham
The Guardian, 8 December 1998

Richard Virenque's phenomenal popularity in France was largely born of television's need to create Tour de France stars. This July, however, the soap opera in which Virenque had starred for six years turned into cycling's worst drugs scandal, but it was still only appropriate that his retirement was announced live on television.

The fact that it was Virenque's brother Lionel, who has been in charge of finding him a place in a team for next year, who broke the news, has led to speculation that the move is a bluff aimed at shocking a team sponsor into backing France's most popular cyclist. Virenque has no backer for next season; none is likely to come forward.

His final shot was aimed at heart strings as well as purse strings. "I would like to apologise to the fans. I would like to continue to make you dream, but I am not being given the chance," he said. Virenque's lawyer, Gilbert Collard, added that his client "is a chap who functions wholly on friendship, and he cannot live with the feeling that he is considered a liar".

The declaration has shocked the wider French public who have not followed the finer contortions of the Festina scandal as it has unfolded since July 8. Virenque will take on the status of a martyr for the public who have lined the roads of France each July waving flags and banners bearing his name.

Next year the banners will ask, as they did last July after he and the Festina team were thrown off the race: why Virenque and not the others?

The answer to that question is that Virenque has chosen the wrong course of action since the scandal broke, when the car carrying the Festina team's drugs to the start of the Tour was stopped by customs on the Franco- Belgian border. His line has been consistent: he is a victim, the affair is a plot, he has never taken drugs.

Virenque has seemed increasingly isolated as teammates and team helpers have confessed one by one to using or providing the drugs. He has always been criticised by his fellow cyclists for behaving as if the Tour de France is his personal fiefdom.

That arrogance turned into a deluded state of mind that was cruelly mocked by France's satirical television show *Les*

Guignols. Their Virenque puppet has several syringes sticking out of his body, but he maintains that they have been put in "without his knowledge by his own free will", which perfectly apes the incongruity of his defence.

This went beyond parody last week when, having been told by the prosecutor investigating the Festina case that lab tests showed he took drugs, Virenque stated, "My name has been cleared."

Virenque won only 12 races in his eight-year career and focused his efforts largely on the Tour, taking four straight wins in the King of the Mountains prize.

For the French public Virenque equalled the Tour. The link was symbolised when he received a fraternal hug from the race director, Jean-Marie Leblanc, the morning after he had been thrown off the race over the drugs allegations.

ON YER BIKE

The Guardian, 17 July 1999

The Tour de France continues to attract a bizarre collection of eccentrics. This week the Italian pin-up of the cycling world, Mario Cipollini (whose name, incidentally, means "little onions") started the Tour's ninth stage dressed as Caesar to celebrate the Roman emperor's 2,099th birthday. This, we add, is a man who keeps a picture of Pamela Anderson on his handlebars to increase testosterone levels and boost his performance. His team were promptly fined \$5,000 for wearing unsanctioned uniforms and Cipollini, hampered by his toga, crashed out of the race.

ARMSTRONG'S GIANT LEAP

The world's toughest race came easy to the Tour de France leader compared with his fight against cancer
by William Fotheringham
The Guardian, 24 July 1999

When Lance Armstrong won his first Tour de France stage at Verdun in 1993 a journalist asked him where he was aiming for, given that his namesake Neil had made it to the moon. The young Texan, already turning heads with his cocksure personality and utterly focused racing style, modestly replied: "Mars".

Two and a half years ago, when Armstrong was diagnosed with testicular cancer which required immediate surgery, France, its Tour, the Champs-Élysées and the yellow jersey might as well all have been on another planet. Yet tomorrow, in a sporting and medical miracle, he is set to ride into Paris as winner of the Tour de France.

By any standards, even compared with men who have not had cancer, it will be one of the biggest Tour wins in recent years. Armstrong has defeated the time-trial and mountain specialists on their home terrain in crushing style and has exuded confidence, which has extended to his mainly American US Postal Service team.

There is every chance that today he will extend his lead to the greatest margin since Bernard Hinault's 14min 34sec in 1981. He already leads Fernando Escartin by a bigger margin than Miguel Indurain achieved in any of his five Tour wins.

The journey has been remarkable. No endurance athlete has ever recovered from cancer as advanced as Armstrong's, including surgery and chemotherapy, and returned to dominate an event as lengthy and demanding as the Tour. Once he left the Saint David hospital in Indianapolis, determined to continue his career as a cyclist, he was in uncharted waters.

"I'm totally confused. I'm going completely into the unknown. A comeback like this has never been attempted. I don't know, my oncologists don't know and obviously the sport doesn't know," he said when he set up his base in Nice at the end of 1997. Tellingly, he had no idea how much furniture to buy: he had no idea how long he would last in professional cycling. He had announced his cancer to the world in a telephone press conference at the start of October

1996; by the end of the month he was weak from chemotherapy, had lost his hair and bore the scars of surgery to remove
lesions from his brain, abdomen and lungs.

"Initially, in the first two weeks, I thought I might die,
but at the point where they discovered the lesions on my
brain I was prepared to die."

STILL BITTER

Armstrong's comeback has always begged one question:
why should anyone want to attempt to return to the most
demanding endurance sport in the world when they have just
cheated death?

He has recalled the time he was diagnosed. "I was scared
that I was going to die, and I was scared that I would lose my
career. I'm not sure what I thought first: 'I'll never race again'
or 'I'm going to die'. That's why it makes sense."

There were other motivations: the fact that a successful
comeback would prove to the cancer community that it was
possible to combat the disease has been crucial to Armstrong.
In addition, once he was healthy again he was seized with the
desire to prove to a sceptical European cycling establishment
that he could return to his previous level.

He is still bitter at the way he was treated by European
teams during his illness. The Cofidis squad, who hired him

just before his diagnosis, attempted to renegotiate his contract downwards as he lay in hospital. Other teams simply did not want to pay him anything like the salary he earned before he became an invalid.

"I was talking to Roger Legeay, the manager of Chris Boardman's team," Armstrong has recalled. "He told me what I was expecting was 'the money of a big rider'. Teams think if I get sick again it will be bad publicity. There is no precedent for what I went through, maybe I'm naive or stupid, but I would have thought that people would want to be part of the story."

He is still bitter about the lack of belief in what he has achieved. On Wednesday, replying to the newspaper *Le Monde*'s story on the fact that minute traces of a corticosteroid had been found in his urine, he said: "This is the story of someone who was not given any chance, everyone said I could not come back. I saw the same mentality when I wanted to find a team, and no one wanted me because they said it was not possible."

There have been false starts in the past two years as Armstrong became "completely terrified that the illness was coming back". In March he left the Paris–Nice stage race and was on the point of quitting. Several weeks of monastic seclusion in North Carolina prompted another rethink, and that marked the start of the upward trajectory which has taken him to the verge of victory in this Tour.

The principal pointer towards his current performance was Armstrong's fourth place in the Tour of Spain in September last year, after which he reflected that even racing in the Madrid sierra in hail and snow was nothing like as bad as being treated for cancer. He had never climbed mountains with the ease he showed then, but during his illness his physique had changed, with the loss of the broad swimmer's shoulders which were the product of triathlons he raced in his youth.

He has another explanation: "I was half dead and was put back together by the best doctors in the world. Perhaps the illness was there for a while and I was training and living with it. Perhaps when I got rid of it, that helped me. You can imagine if you have an advanced form of cancer what it does to your body."

Inspires awe

He has also pointed out: "To race and suffer, that's hard. But that's not being laid out in a hospital bed in Indianapolis with a catheter hanging out of my chest, with platinum pumping into my veins, throwing up for 24 hours straight for five days, taking a two-week break and doing it again. We've all heard the expression 'what doesn't kill you makes you stronger' and that's exactly it."

Perhaps the same will be true of the world's greatest bike race. Even after the drug scandals, police inquiries and revelations of the past year, the Tour de France still inspires awe at the physical and mental efforts it demands of its participants, from the yellow jersey to the *lanterne rouge*.

Its attraction for its international crowds which, on the evidence of this year's roadsides, are still as warm as ever in their affections, has always been founded on the fact that most people ride a bike and can have some idea of the physical effort involved. One thing sets this year's race apart from the 85 that have preceded it: only Armstrong and the rest of the cancer community truly know what it has taken to win.

CHAPTER SEVEN
HIGH STAKES

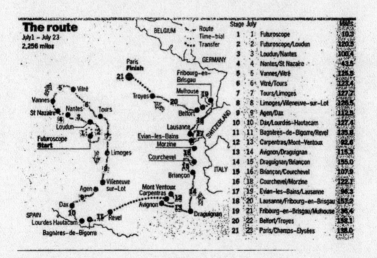

AMERICAN FACES UPHILL BATTLE FOR HERO'S HOMECOMING

by Martin Kettle

The Guardian, 30 July 2001

After three weeks of epic pedalling, expending up to 10,000 calories of energy a day, Lance Armstrong finally made it to the front page of his country's most prestigious newspaper at the weekend. Hours before the Texan's latest and arguably greatest win in his sport's most prestigious race, the *New York Times* finally recognised his Tour de France achievements by putting his picture on the front of Saturday's edition.

It was a rare moment of wider national recognition for a sports star whose Tour exploits may make him the talk of continental Europe each summer but whose deeds are followed from across the Atlantic by only a niche group of fans, with Armstrong eclipsed in the US media by the latest home-run heroics of the baseball sluggers and the upcoming gridiron training camps. The *Times* picture told a symbolic story. It showed Armstrong going flat out in the yellow jersey, hunched over his handlebars as he imposingly added a

249

fourth stage win to his 2001 Tour de France tally in Friday's 37.9-mile individual time trial from Montluçon to St-Amand-Montron, thereby setting the seal on his triple triumph in *le grand bouclé*.

Armstrong's third successive triumph on the Champs-Élysées yesterday, together with Greg LeMond's treble a decade or so ago, means that Americans have won the Tour six times in the past 15 years. It is a record that only cycling-crazy Spain can rival. What is more, those 15 years have seen not a single Frenchman crowned on a winner's podium, even in 1989 when LeMond edged Laurent Fignon off the No 1 spot in the cruellest last-day finish ever likely in the Tour.

But while the attention of Europe remains loyally fixed on the Tour despite professional cycling's doping scandals, Americans still seem to be taking only passing notice of the achievements of Armstrong and his US Postal Service team.

PUT ME BACK ON MY BIKE: IN SEARCH OF TOM SIMPSON

(William Fotheringham, Yellow Jersey Press)

by Tim Moore

The Observer, 11 August 2002

Tom Simpson should have been a definitively British hero: the miner's son taking on the French at their own game, the first Anglo-Saxon to lead the world's ultimate physical contest, the suicidally defiant last words rasped out on the ghastly wasteland of Mont Ventoux, words that give William Fotheringham's affecting biography its title.

But even as the roadside resuscitation attempts continued on that scorched and airless afternoon 25 years ago, a discovery was made that would complicate the obituaries. The Tour de France doctor felt tubes of pills in Simpson's pocket, and an autopsy later confirmed that amphetamines and alcohol compounded the effects of heat exhaustion on a day when café thermometers burst across Provence.

Whenever the Tour goes up Ventoux, as it did again last month, the Simpson tragedy is retold. A toddler in 1967, Fotheringham still found himself in the man's shadow in the 1980s, riding as an amateur against the old pro who had been Simpson's Tour room-mate. Interviewed in his Paignton bike shop, Colin Lewis talks of the two Italians who visited their hotel, handing over a small case containing what Simpson winkingly called his "year's supply of Mickey Finns" in exchange for £800 – a huge sum, almost four times Lewis's annual retainer from his team. The night before the Ventoux stage there was another visitor, Simpson's agent, delivering an ultimatum: get into the top five or pay the financial price for the rest of the year, which for a sportsman three months off 30 effectively meant for the rest of his life. Weakened by diarrhoea – every night the mechanics had to hose down his bike – he had already slipped to seventh. There can be few more haunting photographs than the one of Simpson moments before his final collapse: the distant gaze more wistful than agonised, a man resigned to his fate after a fruitless last throw of the dice.

Blame Simpson, his agent, the Italians – but while you're about it, blame the Tour organisers, whose inhuman itinerary included 360km daily stages and whose draconian stipulations prevented Simpson receiving water from his team car, so compelling Lewis to rehydrate his leader with whatever he could seize from roadside bars: sometimes Coke, sometimes cognac.

No British cyclist before or since has come close to matching Simpson's achievements, and it is Fotheringham's contention that Simpson succeeded because, setting off for the Continent in 1959 with £100 in his panniers, he made a point of leaving his homeland's amateur ideals behind. "The thing is not the position you finished," he wrote to a friend back in England, "but how much you make." To extract the full market value of his 1965 world championship success he raced 18 times throughout Europe in three weeks, covering 12,000 miles behind the wheel between events.

Fotheringham reveals Simpson as a meticulous professional in a ruthlessly professional sport, constructing his own saddle to a design now universal, and following a diet that included 10lbs of carrots a day. A virtuoso of the PR stunt, Simpson was happy to indulge the French press by posing in bowler hat and brolly; on the morning of his death he obliged the photographers by larking about in a rowing boat at the stage's Marseille start. Drugs were simply another aspect of that professionalism, ubiquitous since the inaugural 1903 Tour and banned only the year before Simpson's death.

IF THIS YEAR'S TOUR DE FRANCE IS 100 PER CENT CLEAN THEN THAT WILL CERTAINLY BE A FIRST

by Matt Seaton and David Adam

The Guardian, 3 July 2003

One hundred years ago, the first Tour de France was completed by its winner Maurice Garin at an average speed of 16mph (26 kmph). Considering that stages then were often hundreds of kilometres long and run continuously through day and night, it was an amazing achievement. Today, of course, an averagely fit cyclist on a touring holiday would have little trouble matching Garin's pace.

Bike technology has improved: first, steel frames became lighter, with derailleur gears, better brakes and stronger wheels; then, more recently, aluminium, titanium and carbon-fibre components have shaved still more valuable grammes off the bikes that racers have to push over the passes of the Alps and Pyrenees.

Diet and training methods, too, have evolved out of ignorance and superstition into sciences in their own right. In recent years, isotonic drinks, carbo-loading, heart-rate monitors and power cranks (which measure a cyclist's output in wattage) have brought to the starting line a new breed of clinically prepared athletes.

So it is hardly surprising that speeds have increased since Garin's day. By 1959, when the great Spaniard Federico Bahamontes won, the average speed was up to 22mph, a figure that was scarcely improved upon for several decades. But by the late 1990s, the *peloton* (main field of riders) had accelerated dramatically, past 25mph. To put this in perspective, an elite amateur race on a flat circuit might expect to average that speed for an hour or so; Tour professionals sustain that pace for three weeks and the best part of 4,000km (2,500 miles).

How on earth is it done? The answer, according to five-times Tour winner, Jacques Anquetil, is that no one can expect pros to race "on mineral water alone". In the 1960s, Anquetil's little helper was *l'amphet* (amphetamine), but in pharmaceutical products – as with bike manufacture and training methods – the technology has moved on. That 1998, in which the Tour recorded its fastest-ever average speed, nudging 26mph, was also the year of the greatest doping scandal was certainly unfortunate … but could you call it a coincidence?

The amphetamines of Anquetil's era worked by acting on the brain, enabling riders to ignore the pain of effort and so push themselves harder. They were not strictly performance-enhancing because they did not alter the cyclist's physiological ability. That came later, in the 70s, with the appearance of anabolic steroids. Clenbuterol, nandrolone and epitestosterone

made cyclists more muscular and stronger, but again performance gains were modest. Muscle mass is a mixed blessing
for a cyclist: useful perhaps for explosive sprints, but of
limited value for long mountain climbs where aerobic capacity is more important. An odd side-effect of steroid abuse
was that "road rash" – the deep grazes sustained in a crash –
took longer to heal. In 1988, Pedro Delgado tested positive
for probenecid, which interferes with chemicals the kidneys
secrete, and aroused a suspicion that he was using it as a
masking agent for steroid use. Probenecid had been banned
by the International Olympic Committee (IOC), but not
yet by the Union Cycliste Internationale (UCI). Delgado's
victory in the Tour that year stood, despite near-universal
scepticism.

By then, steroids were being overtaken as the *dope de
choix* by the most significant development in the history
of performance-enhancing drug use: a synthetic version of
erythropoietin (EPO), a hormone naturally produced by the
kidneys that stimulates red blood cell production. More red
blood cells mean more oxygen-carrying capacity and a higher
aerobic threshold – the holy grail for cyclists. Training at altitude for several months has similar benefits but they are eaten
up with the first races of the season and the body returns to
normal – only EPO will go on working all season long.

A normal elite athlete will have a haematocrit (a measure of the blood's oxygen carrying capacity) level of around 44 per cent. With altitude training, this might rise to 48 per cent. With EPO, levels of over 50 per cent became obtainable. But there are risks: the blood can become so thick that heart failure can occur. EPO has been implicated in the deaths of as many as 20 elite athletes, most of them cyclists, in recent years. "In the past, the anti-doping system was more reactive than proactive," says Olivier Rabin, science director of the Montreal-based World Anti-Doping Agency (Wada). "If you go back to the abuse of anabolic steroids in the 60s and 70s, it took (until the early 80s) to get a reliable testing process in place. In the case of EPO, it was prohibited very soon after it came on the market around in 1987 – the IOC banned it in 1989."

But banning a substance is little use without a reliable test. With EPO, it was not until the Sydney Olympics in 2000 that such a test was in place (the problem was to distinguish between natural and synthetic versions of EPO). Before then, all the UCI could do was demand blood tests that permitted riders a haematocrit level up to 50 per cent. The message appeared to be that they could use EPO with impunity – provided it was medically regulated and in moderation. Finally, in 1998, humble customs officers succeeded in busting the sport where its governing body had failed: the

Festina team *soigneur* was picked up on the French-Belgian border with a carload of EPO and other banned substances days before the start of the Tour.

L'affaire Festina rocked the sport: cyclists were pulled in for questioning by gendarmes during the race; several teams pulled out in protest. In its wake, the IOC convened a conference on anti-doping that established Wada. Wada's strategy now is to be much more aggressive in pursuing tests.

"We maintain regular contact with the pharmaceutical industry so that we learn about substances that are not yet available," says Rabin. "Where blood-doping products are concerned, we have a programme to identify substances that are still in development and derive tests for them."

EPO must now be seen by cyclists as a risky option, but even a rigorous testing regime may not be 100 per cent reliable. The surprise third-placed rider last year, Lithuanian Raimondas Rumsas, has just tested positive for the drug. But he did not last year when his wife was stopped by customs with a large supply of EPO. Rumsas claimed it was for his mother-in-law and, at the time, escaped penalty. As the French press remarked, with that kind of help, Rumsas's mother-in-law could probably win the Tour.

If cycling is entering a post-EPO era, does that mean this year's Tour, which starts on Saturday, is clean? Probably not. The performance benefits of blood-doping products especially will prove just too tempting. Actovegin, a serum extracted from calves's blood, is one substance that was tipped to be the new EPO. In 2000, a French TV crew filmed rubbish being discarded by a member of Lance Armstrong's US Postal team that included packaging for Actovegin. The team was investigated, but said it was for treatment of skin abrasions and a non-competing team member with diabetes; the squad was cleared. Little is known about its properties but Rabin is adamant that it is of no use in blood-doping.

There have been rumours for some years about the use of human growth hormone (HGH). Acting rather like steroids (and so beloved of bodybuilders), its value to cyclists is limited as far as performance goes, but it undoubtedly aids recovery, particularly from injury. Little is known about the potential health hazards of HGH abuse. The anecdotal evidence, though, is comic: one well-known French rider was said to have had to change his shoe size mid-season due to his HGH habit.

Meanwhile, new blood oxygen-carrying technologies are emerging. Scientists in Cambridge have chemically modified human haemoglobin with amino acids from a crocodile's, in a process that could yield a high-quality artificial haemoglobin. Another route might involve the intravenous injection of artificial haemoglobin derived either from bovine sources or by genetic engineering, or of perfluorocarbons (chemicals similar to Teflon), which can function very like haemoglobin by dissolving oxygen and delivering it to body tissues. Inert chemicals, they would be practically unmeasurable in blood and urine tests; only gas chromatography of expired air might detect their presence.

For some time now, in fact, Wada has been warning that we are on the verge of seeing the first genetically modified athlete. Several pharmaceutical companies are developing ways to give patients a new copy of the gene that produces EPO. The techniques are not yet ready for human trials, but when they are, cyclists will probably be among the first to abuse the process, says Bengt Saltin, head of the Muscle Research Centre at Copenhagen University and an expert on drugs in sport. "For this Tour de France, it's not an option, but it will be a real threat within the next five or 10 years." Animal tests have shown the gene can be easily inserted, and that it readily produces EPO that, unlike the synthetic drug taken by the Festina team, would be impossible to distinguish from a cyclist's own. The problem is that the gene works too well. Baboons given EPO gene therapy had to have their blood regularly diluted to keep them alive after their haematocrit level soared from 40 per cent to 75 per cent in under three months. "When it comes to the EPO gene, they know how to do it and it works well in the monkeys, but they have no way of shutting it off," says Saltin.

Wada is already working on ways to detect rogue gene therapy. "Always the objective is to get one step ahead of the cheats," says Rabin. "I don't want to say that in two or three years there will be no more doping, but we are certainly winning some battles."

TOO-FAST FOOD LEAVES A NASTY AFTERTASTE

by William Fotheringham
The Guardian, 9 July 2003

When almost 200 cyclists are unleashed on to the roads of France, etiquette might seem a minor consideration. But when the 23-year-old Frenchman Anthony Geslin went clear of the *peloton* at the feeding area yesterday, he was breaking an unwritten rule: the point where the cyclists gather their small cotton bags of energy food is sacrosanct. "Grilling the *ravito*", as cycling slang has it, is strictly a no-no.

This is nothing to do with the fact that lunch is a sacred ritual in France, but simply because collecting the *musettes* – done non-stop in the same way that Auden's night mail scooped up mailbags from the lineside stands – is an operation best done at a sensible pace. To illustrate the point, there was a crash in the *zone de ravitaillement* yesterday after Geslin's attack.

Like any community, the *peloton* has its rules. There is the Tour's rule book, restricting activities such as urinating in public and where to collect bottles from the team car, and there are the unwritten conventions that simply make life safer, more pleasant and more remunerative for the cyclists.

Not riding dangerously is the most obvious, although the sprinters interpret that one extremely loosely. If the *ravito* is sacrosanct, so are the collective moments when a large group of riders – usually led by the yellow jersey of the day – collectively decide to suspend hostilities on a quiet stretch of roadside and empty their bladders. The occasion on which Laurent Jalabert lost the yellow jersey in 2000 because a group of riders failed to respect this rule is now known as the pisspot revolution.

The worst crime in the unwritten rule book, says David Millar, is "attacking a yellow jersey when he's crashed or punctured". The *maillot jaune* is accorded great respect: it is the convention that if the wearer wishes to glide forwards in the group, his fellows will slip aside or, if the field is lined out, he will be permitted to enter the string.

The rules revolve around mutual respect, which is why Lance Armstrong famously waited for Jan Ullrich when he crashed on a Pyrenean descent two years ago, rather than taking advantage: Armstrong would expect the same of the German.

It is also why, when two cyclists have escaped together, and one takes the yellow jersey at the stage finish, he will permit his co-escapee to have the stage win. The tactic that arouses the most ire is "wheelsucking": feigning fatigue in a breakaway, then discovering your strength in the finish sprint.

"There's less and less respect in the bunch," says Millar, shaking his head at the antics of what he ironically terms "the younger generation". He explains: "There are fewer and fewer windows of opportunity to get clear of the bunch, fewer times when the pace is slow, so a small minority will take advantage."

Punishment is collective: verbal warnings in several languages, then the mistrust and retribution of the *peloton* for repeat offenders, which is why Geslin may not be permitted to show his face again on this Tour. His lunchtime break may cost him dear.

TOUR ETIQUETTE
* Never attack if the *peloton* is near, in or leaving the feeding area.
* Never attack when a large number are having a toilet stop.
* Share cans of coke and bottles of mineral water.
* Never attack when the race leader crashes or punctures.

* Always contribute to an escape, then win the sprint.
* Slow up and let the race leader go where he wants if appropriate.
* Never poke your nose between a sprinter and a lead-out man.
* Never get mixed up in the sprint unless you are fully committed.
* If two of you escape, and you have the yellow jersey, let your fellow escapee win the stage.
* Never attack in a tunnel.

CYCLE DRAMA

The Tour de France is compulsive watching, and not only for the tight shorts and incomprehensible rules
by Zoe Williams
The Guardian, 15 July 2003

People always say that yellow jerseys are born, not made – reaching that summit of human attainment is written on to your genetic imprint. You'll find it filed under "spirit of a champion" and "nice big thighs". There is no amount of training that will make heroes of the unworthy. And I suppose this is true of all sport, as well as ballet, mathematical genius and the ability to get on well with any given dog, but it seems especially, superlatively true of the Tour de France.

It is impossible to feel anything but the deepest admiration for these cyclists, even while you don't understand exactly what they're engaged in. (The only two people I know who can explain the rules are both in France, chasing the race on bikes. I think it's fair to say they won't catch it, since they started a week late and keep getting stoned, but that's an index of the pull of this sport – to comprehend it is to follow it all the way. Well, some of the way.)

Cycling has a very sophisticated relationship with modernity – it's not Luddite; no one would ever eschew technological advances in design, in favour of a crap one with wooden wheels. But the very act of racing on bicycles when motorised transport exists suggests a critical distance from progress – an environmental concern, possibly, but more importantly a comprehension that physical struggle is an end in itself, and that to etch it out of endeavour diminishes man's Olympian spirit. Plus, I like their tight shorts.

And really, even their cheating has an old-world charm; one racer had someone hide in the bushes and pass him a lead pipe on the way down a hill, to speed his descent. It's got everything – ingenuity, physics, human frailty, friendship and shrubbery. Having said that, most Tour cheating isn't about gravity at all, it's about drugs. They are inveterate caners, the racers, and always have been. In 1924, Henri Pélissier said to a journalist: "That's cocaine to go in our eyes, chloroform for our gums, and do you want to see the pills? We keep going on dynamite. In the evenings we dance around our rooms instead of sleeping." I find this pretty tickling – where all other athletes roll over in shame or denial when they're accused of chemical enhancement, cyclists say: "Well, we're engaged in a feat of epic proportions. This is mankind against nature. Of course we're going to take drugs!"

This element – that while this is a battle between men, the greatest adversary is the mountain – is echoed in the altruistic codes of the race. There is a huge amount of sacrifice built into the process. Someone rides in front, breaking the wind for the champion; someone else rides alongside, and holds his bike steady while he has a drink; you're not allowed to overtake while someone's having a wee; the packs they travel in epitomise the noblest kind of human cooperation, since they are all elite cyclists, these people, and yet they undergo unthinkable pain for the triumph of just one rider.

Even in individual races in velodromes, you see this happening – the races start incredibly sluggishly, since the person who takes the lead will lose all his energy breaking everyone else's wind, and always end up last. So the true starting point of every race is a surrender, which although made unwillingly, is still kind of cute.

But if the riders are the heroes, the bikes are the stars. You always see car adverts stressing the fit of man and machine, but nobody really fits with their car. The shape, the efficiency (better than a salmon's, apparently), the simplicity of a bike is really the endpoint of Cartesian perfection. This is why Beckett had such a thing about the eroticism of the bicycle (in *More Pricks Than Kicks*, the hero rejects a lady suitor in favour of a bike) – it's not because you'd want to have sex with a bike (silly), it's because the perfect clunk-click of symbiosis that people associate with nooky is completely expressed in the relationship between man and bicycle. If the horse represents slavery and the car represents indolent consumption, the bike represents nothing but the honest profit of inventive genius.

My boyfriend would like to point out that when Jesus rode into Jerusalem, he used an ass because a horse was too indicative of mankind's arrogance. And yet, the ass is still enslaved; if bikes had been invented, he feels sure the Godhead would have ridden one of those. I'd counter that, since God is omnipotent, if he'd wanted Christ to have a bike he would have fixed it for someone to invent it sooner. But these are theological matters. Incidentally, the closest Beckett ever got to explaining *Waiting for Godot* was when he referred to "a veteran racing cyclist, bald, a 'stayer', recurrent placeman in town-to-town and national championships, Christian name elusive, surname Godeau, pronounced, of course, no differently from Godot". So, not only are they handy for getting about, these lovely machines can also unlock a completely impenetrable work of literature.

For all these reasons, and more that haven't occurred to me, the Tour de France is a beautiful phenomenon. Issues that befuddle other sports – sponsorship, cash, drugs, even competition – are irrelevant. You could watch it all day, every day. And you don't much care who wins, so long as someone does.

TOUR DE FRANCE: THE SCANDALS THAT ROCKED CYCLING

by Matt Rendell
The Observer, 31 2004

Competing on the open road is not without its hazards and the thugs who showered Lance Armstrong with spittle on Alpe d'Huez last July were part of an unfortunate tradition. The winner of the first Tour de France in 1904 [actually 1903], Maurice Garin, was attacked by a spectator the following year. "If I'm not murdered before we reach Paris," he said, "I'll win again." So he did, only to see his victory annulled four months later after an inquest found that he had covered part of the route by train. The first four riders in the GC team, including Garin's younger brother César (third), were disqualified and numerous others were fined for illegal teamwork, travelling by car and taking short cuts. Tour director Henri Desgrange wrote: "The Tour is over and its second edition will also, I fear, be its last." The fifth-placed rider, 20-year-old Henri Cornet, was eventually declared the winner. He remains the youngest Tour winner. Garin temporarily quit the sport.

But the Tour would go on to greater and worse things: in 1950, French crowds despaired as the all-powerful Italians rode towards their third consecutive Tour win. On the Aspin pass in the Pyrenees, bottle tops and stones rained down on the Italians, before the road itself was blocked. French riders protected their vanquishers and race director Jacques Goddet leapt into the fray brandishing a walking stick to keep the aggressors at bay. Only police intervention allowed the stage to be completed. Gino Bartali, the 1948 winner, raced away to victory and his team-mate Fiorenzo Magni took over the yellow jersey. However, both forfeited their chances of overall victory when their team withdrew later that evening, fearing further incidents.

The most notorious example of spectator–athlete interaction in Tour history took place in 1975. Unbeatable over any terrain, Eddy Merckx tyrannised his peers to a degree that even Armstrong has never achieved. This translated into five Tour wins in five starts between 1969 and 1974. In 1973, however, he publicly snubbed the Tour after winning a historic double of the tours of Italy and Spain in the spring. The decision of the world's most famous Belgian to skip the Tour enraged many of its followers.

This, coupled with Merckx's overwhelming domination of the sport, drove one French onlooker to an act of insanity in 1975. After winning stage six, a short time trial, to take the race lead, Merckx cemented his advantage by taking a second time trial on stage nine. Then, on the notorious climb to Puy de Dôme, his energy levels began to flag. Lagging behind his greatest rivals, eventual winner Bernard Thévenet and 1976 champion Lucien van Impe, Merckx was trying to bridge the gap when a fist dramatically appeared from the crowd, striking him in the kidneys. Doubled up by the blow, Merckx finished the stage winded. He conceded less than a minute, but his attempt to win an unprecedented sixth Tour was fatally damaged. The following day, the perpetrator of the blow was waiting at the stage start; he was arrested after Merckx identified him, but was later released without charge.

Matt Rendell is author of *A Significant Other: Riding the Tour with Lance Armstrong* (Weidenfeld).

MERCKX: LANCE THE ATTACKER

William Fotheringham hears the view of the most successful cyclist ever on the making of a Tour legend

The Observer, 24 July 2005

On an early June afternoon, the day after Eddy Merckx's sixtieth birthday, the greatest cyclist ever rode for 40 miles near his home in the suburbs of Brussels with Lance Armstrong, the man who has inherited the "cannibal's" status as the most redoubtable cyclist of his generation. "He told me his plan for ending his career and made it clear to me that he did not contemplate being defeated in this Tour," said Merckx. "He said, 'Another seven weeks and it's over.'"

Like Merckx, Armstrong is not a man who has ever expected defeat and, as the American predicted to the old champion, he has come to the final day of his final Tour with his seventh victory in the bag.

As happened last year after Armstrong's sixth victory, the Texan will be compared with the "cannibal", who dominated cycling between 1968 and 1977, winning 476 professional races in a 13-season career. Merckx won five Tours de France to Armstrong's probable seven, but he missed the race in 1973 to pursue other races and took a total of six wins in the other great Tours, Italy and Spain, neither of which Armstrong has won.

The "cannibal" still has his distinguished air, his high cheekbones that some compared with those of a sphinx, and he is as combative as ever. Speaking to *The Observer* en route to this year's finale, Merckx was as keen to fight his corner as might have been expected of the most successful professional cyclist of all time. "I was a more aggressive rider than Armstrong. I would attack more often. He waits for the other guys, then counter-attacks."

Merckx acknowledged that Armstrong shares his insatiable hunger for victory "particularly last year, when he won five stages", but added that the Texan "races more in the style of [fellow five-times winners] Jacques Anquetil or Miguel Indurain". "Master Jacques" and "Big Mig" were noted for targeting certain stages, whereas the Merckx way was to attempt to win every stage.

The "cannibal" feels that the way he and Armstrong raced makes comparisons invidious. "The two eras are totally different. I raced from 1 February to 31 October every year, competed for everything. When [like Armstrong] you are the best rider in the bunch and contest one race a year ..." Merckx is too polite to say it, but the message is similar to that of another five-time winner, Bernard Hinault, who said: "With Armstrong's racing programme, I would still be competing today and so would Eddy."

There are similarities, however. Both have pushed the boundaries of dedication to their sport and both are perfectionists to the point of obsession. Merckx was legendary for getting up in the middle of the night to check his saddle height and had a cellar full of tyres; Armstrong has a workshop with a pile of discarded saddles that have failed to come up to scratch, he reconnoitres every mountain stage and receives constant updates on his rivals.

Merckx does not believe that the way Armstrong races is beneficial for the sport, with its sole emphasis on one race, the Tour de France, putting the rest of the calendar in the shade. "It's not good for cycling, but how else can you race when the Tour is so important?" he said. "The only event that counts is the Tour, it's the only race that all the media go to. It's far more important than it was in my time, but as I see it cycling is more than the Tour de France."

The old champion and budding star first met when Armstrong raced on one of Merckx's bikes at the Barcelona Olympics in 1992. Subsequently, Merckx supplied bikes to the Texan's first professional team, Motorola, and the pair became close, particularly after Merckx's son, Axel – who will finish the Tour this year for the Davitamon-Lotto team – joined the squad. "Eddy told me I could win a Tour de France some day, but that I needed to lose weight," wrote Armstrong in his autobiography *It's Not About the Bike*.

The book has a photograph of Merckx, corpulent and suited, visiting a lean, frail-looking Armstrong in hospital when the Texan was in remission from testicular cancer in late 1996. Armstrong insisted that the "cannibal" accompany him on his first bike ride after the illness.

"He was determined to come back to what he had been and I was impressed," Merckx said recently in an interview with *L'Équipe*. "No one believed in him at the time. Even I would never have thought he was capable of coming back and winning the Tour de France."

The friendship between the two has become tense in public on one occasion only, when Merckx accused Armstrong of racing to make Axel lose in a big one-day event, the Liège–Bastogne–Liège, but the "cannibal" feels that Armstrong has been misunderstood.

"The press has often been unjust where he is concerned," he said. "What is said about him has to be measured. Before his cancer he had already shown immense class, becoming world champion in Oslo in 1993, ahead of Indurain, who is not just a nobody.

"He didn't transform himself thanks to the grace of God, but by building on all his setbacks, by training like hell and sorting out his lifestyle. To begin with he ate anything, drank quite a few beers, even before a major race. The cancer slimmed him down, but it also weakened him, I believe, quite a bit, and that's why he has limited what he does to the Tour de France. Without the cancer he would have had a racing record far beyond the norm."

As of this afternoon, when Armstrong rides up the Champs-Élysées to win his seventh Tour, a new problem will confront him: dealing with retirement. Like many great athletes, Merckx had difficulty adapting to life outside sport – he famously said that at one point he could envisage no other existence than that of a professional cyclist – and he has some inkling of what awaits Armstrong.

"I stopped because I was tired of always racing," said Merckx. "It wasn't difficult for me to stop. I was mentally exhausted. But after that you need to find new goals, new things to aim for." In Merckx's case, he put his energy into his bike factory, but it took him several years, in which his weight ballooned.

This week, even as he raced his last mountain stage, his last hill-top finish and watched his team defend the yellow jersey for the last time, Armstrong said that he has yet to feel any emotion about leaving racing behind; he was neither sad nor happy at the thought. Quite how the most competitively minded and obsessively dedicated cyclist since Merckx will cope remains to be seen.

His old mentor is optimistic, feeling that cancer has given Armstrong contact with the everyday world that many athletes lack. "I don't know if Armstrong will find it hard to get into normal life. You can't really compare our cases," said Merckx. "He is a racer, too, but he has had cancer and has found other things in life which are important. He will find new goals to occupy his time without too much trouble."

TOUR GREATS

Lance Armstrong

Nationality: American

Tours started: 11

Tour de France wins: 6 (1999, 2000, 2001, 2002, 2003, 2004)

Biggest winning margin: 7min 37sec (1999)

Tour de France stage wins: 21

Days spent in yellow jersey: 81

World championship wins: 1 (1993)

Miguel Indurain

Nationality: Spanish

Tours started: 12

Tour de France wins: 5 (1991, 1992, 1993, 1994, 1995)

Biggest winning margin: 5min 39sec (1994)

Tour de France stage wins: 12

Days spent in yellow jersey: 60

World championship wins:

Bernard Hinault

Nationality: French

Tours started: 9

Tour de France wins: 5 (1978, 1979, 1981, 1982, 1985)

Biggest winning margin: 14min 34sec (1981)

Tour de France stage wins: 28

Days spent in yellow jersey: 78

World championship wins: 1 (1980)

Eddy Merckx

Nationality: Belgian

Tours started: 7

Tour de France wins: 5 (1969, 1970, 1971, 1972, 1974)

Biggest winning margin: 17min 54sec (1969)

Tour de France stage wins: 34

Days spent in yellow jersey: 96

World championship wins: 3 (1967, 1971, 1974)

Jacques Anquetil

Nationality: French

Tours started: 8

Tour de France wins: 5 (1957, 1961, 1962, 1963, 1964)

Biggest winning margin: 14min 56sec (1957)

Tour de France stage wins: 15

Days spent in yellow jersey: 51

World championship wins:

ARMSTRONG RIDES INTO HISTORY WITH SEVENTH TOUR WIN

by Richard Williams

The Guardian, 25 July 2005

Lance Armstrong, the cancer survivor whose yellow wristbands are worn around the world by some 40 million contributors to his Livestrong charity, rode off the Champs-Élysées and into sporting history last night after fulfilling his ambition to become the first man to win the Tour de France seven times.

Armstrong was breaking a record he set a year ago, when he took himself clear of the four men – Jacques Anquetil, Eddy Merckx, Bernard Hinault and Miguel Indurain – who had won the race five times. But the real record was established long ago, when he proved that it was possible to survive radical treatment for cancer and go on to victory in the world's most gruelling sporting event.

In the course of his seven consecutive victories, Armstrong pedalled more than 15,000 miles up and down the Alps and the Pyrenees, through the vineyards of Bordeaux and Provence, and past innumerable chateaux and sunflower fields. At 33, nine years after his testicular cancer was diagnosed, he is taking his trophies and his record into retirement.

His career has been studded with incident and controversy, and yesterday's rainstorms as the race approached the finish in Paris almost cost him his concluding appearance on the podium.

LANDIS SACKED AFTER TEST IS CONFIRMED

by Denis Campbell
The Observer, 6 August 2006

Tour de France winner Floyd Landis was sacked by his team after the back-up doping sample taken during the race confirmed that he had excessive levels of testosterone in his body.

The 30-year-old American is now set to become the first winner in the 103-year history of cycling's biggest event to be stripped of his title over a drugs scandal. Phonak, the Swiss team, immediately dismissed the disgraced rider "without notice for violating the team's internal code of ethics".

The Union Cycliste Internationale said that Landis's "B" sample confirmed the initial "adverse analytical finding" for a level of the male hormone that was higher than the rules allow. UCI lawyer Philippe Verbiest said Landis would continue to be classed as the champion until disciplinary proceedings had been resolved. Landis issued a statement again protesting his innocence. He plans to appeal and take legal action to try to clear his name.

OBITUARY: FÉLIX LÉVITAN

A natural showman, he brought success to the Tour de France
by William Fotheringham
The Guardian, 3 April 2007

Félix Lévitan, who has died aged 95, began his working life running errands at a Paris cycling magazine and rose to become an organiser of the Tour de France for 40 years. He laid the foundations for the event's rapid growth in the late 1980s and invented two integral parts of the Tour's make-up: the grand finale on the Champs-Élysées and the polka-dot "redpeas" jersey awarded to the race's King of the Mountains.

Lévitan was born into a family of Jewish shoemakers in Paris's 15th arrondissement. His brother was an amateur cycle racer, and together they tried to hang on to the best professionals of the day as they trained in the Bois de Boulogne or the Longchamp racetrack, before, at the age of 16, he began working as a telephonist on *Le Pédale* magazine.

His first published piece was entitled "Vouloir, c'est pouvoir" – "If you want to, you can" – which he said was "not very good". But more accurately, he described the title as his personal credo. Subsequently Lévitan worked for the newspapers *L'Intransigeant* – first thing in the morning – and, in the evening, its rival *L'Auto*.

Even though Lévitan described himself as "appallingly irreligious", he did not escape the round-ups of Jews during the Nazi occupation of 1940–44, and he was interned in the Cherche-Midi military prison in Paris. His wife Geneviève managed to arrange his transfer to Dijon, without which he was certain he would have ended up in a concentration camp.

When the Paris press was restructured after the liberation, he was appointed head of sport at the *Parisien Libéré* newspaper, and when a joint team was appointed by the *Parisien* and its sister newspaper *L'Équipe* to run the first postwar Tour in 1947, Lévitan found his true vocation. While *L'Équipe*'s head Jacques Goddet concentrated on the sporting side – devising the course and the entry criteria, tweaking the rules to liven up the event – Lévitan made the race pay.

The Tour had originally been devised as a means of creating exclusive copy for the newspaper that ran it, but Lévitan turned it into a commercial enterprise in its own right by expanding the garish cavalcade of advertising vehicles and making stage towns pay heavily for the privilege of hosting starts and finishes. The race's prologue time trial was instigated in 1967 as a way of getting more cash out of the town hosting the "Grand Départ". Most importantly, he understood the significance of selling television rights, which are now what pays the race's way.

Small and dapper, with a frosty smile, Lévitan was formally appointed joint organiser in 1962, and he copied the dictatorial style of his and Goddet's predecessor, Henri Desgrange. The eight-times stage winner from Yorkshire Barry Hoban recalled one occasion on which he had won an intermediate prize: it was confirmed by the judge, only for Lévitan to reverse the verdict. "You can't do that," expostulated the cyclist. "My dear Barry, I have every right," came the implacable reply.

In 1975 came Lévitan's two masterstrokes. One was the decision to make the best mountain climber wear a red spotted jersey, the "*maillot à pois*", or the "measled vest" as one English writer termed it: the jersey is now one of the race's three major prizes together with the yellow jersey of overall leader and the green jersey worn by the points leader. For that same year's Tour, Lévitan devised the ambitious plan of running the closing stage through the heart of Paris, along the Rue de Rivoli and the banks of the Seine, with the finish on the Champs. The French president Giscard d'Estaing welcomed the idea – and attended the finish – but his police chief restricted the race to a loop up and down the great boulevard, with the riders performing a U-turn before the Arc de Triomphe. The circuit is now the most distinctive feature of the whole event.

Lévitan did not stop there. He began a shortlived women's event alongside the men's Tour, and was the driving force behind the arrival of Colombian cyclists in the event in 1983. His dream was to export the Tour to America, with the race starting in New York and the riders flown across the Atlantic to complete the event in France.

His vision of cycling as a world sport, if not that of a tour of the world, was eventually realised, but an abortive event in the US, the Tour of the Americas, proved his undoing: he was sacked suddenly in 1987 on the grounds that he could not account for the money spent on the event, but later a court ruled the Tour's parent company had no case against him. The recipient of three grades of the *légion d'honneur*, he returned to the race on occasion, but he and his event were never truly reconciled.

His wife predeceased him.

Félix Lévitan, cycle race organiser, born October 12 1911; died February 17 2007

HOW AND WHY TELECOMMUNICATIONS HAVE REVOLUTIONISED TOUR DE FRANCE TACTICS

The Guardian, 6 July 2007

Mobile-phone and radio technology have changed the way the Tour de France is run. Since the mid-1990s, ever-improving communication between the riders and their team leaders has had a huge impact on the tactics employed. When the Tour begins in London tomorrow, two-way radios, TV feeds and mobile phones mean crucial information can be passed to riders. This is especially important in determining how teams and individuals deal with breakaways from the *peloton*.

HOW RIDERS RECEIVE THEIR ORDERS

The two-way radios worn by riders are the size of a credit card and fit into a special pocket sewn into the back of the shorts. A wire goes up under the shirt and an earpiece is taped over one ear. Every team has its own frequency and every rider in the team can hear the message from the car. In the following cars, mobile phones, two-way radio receivers and TVs keep the team leaders, *directeurs sportif*, up to date with what is going on and in touch with their riders.

WITHOUT RADIO CONTACT

If a group breaks away from the *peloton* the riders usually don't know who is in the breakaway. Previously they would have had to wait for information from the race organisers via a blackboard, or drop to the rear of the group to talk to their team.

WITH RADIO CONTACT

Now the team manager can see what has happened on the television. He then speaks to the riders through their transmitters and can instruct them to reel the breakaway back before the gap grows too large. The technology helps teams make quick decisions based on hard evidence, rather than the riders using their own initiative and experience.

CANCELLARA CAPTURES ELATION OF GOLDEN DAY

The Swiss speedster left the huge crowd gasping in a London en fête for the Tour
by Richard Williams
The Guardian, 9 July 2007

Of all the sights and sounds that turned the centre of London into a sun-dappled carnival on Saturday afternoon, perhaps the most extraordinary was the spectacle of French motor-cycle gendarmes leading the Tour de France competitors past the statue of Queen Victoria and into the finishing straight along the Mall. Maybe that explained why no member of the royal family emerged on the balcony of Buckingham Palace to watch the world's greatest free sporting event passing by their front door.

There could have been few other reasons for failing to acknowledge the arrival of the Tour, which started in Britain for the first time in its 104-year history with a prologue time trial over a 7.9km course that began in Whitehall, continued through Hyde Park and finished alongside the John Nash terraces lining the north side of the Mall.

It is thought that more than a million people turned up to watch the event; certainly the course was packed along both sides of the road for its entire length, often four or five deep, while each of several big screens in the park beamed the telecast of the race to an audience big enough for a respectable rock festival.

They had been arriving throughout the morning from all points of the compass. From the west, flotillas of families left their homes in Kingston and Surbiton and trundled through Richmond Park on mountain bikes, heading for a picnic; from the east, squadrons of cycle couriers on stripped-down single-speeds swooped in from Hoxton and Bow; from the south came gnarled road-men wearing the colours of Dulwich Paragon and Catford CC; while the main-line stations on the city's northern rim disgorged fans who had made the rail journey from cycling's heartlands among the Yorkshire dales and the Derbyshire peaks.

Their presence, together with the Tour's well-oiled travelling infrastructure, turned the occasion into perhaps London's happiest mass event since VE Day. As soon as the first rider, Enrico Degano of Italy, was flagged away on the stroke of 3pm by the mayor of London, Ken Livingstone, the whole place became a gigantic velodrome. And it stayed that way until 6.17pm, when Oscar Pereiro crossed the finish line, the last of the 189 riders to surf the course on a moving pulse of cheers.

Allowed to construct a starting order by seeding their riders, the team managers responded to the special nature of the afternoon by backloading their British riders, placing them among the top names. Given the presence of Bradley Wiggins and David Millar among the favourites, the tactic ensured that tension would be maintained until the very last seconds.

Virtually every metre of the course contributed its own piece to the great jigsaw of the day's atmosphere. The riders entered Hyde Park beneath an arch no more than two metres wide, through a funnel of spectators as close to the action as they would be on the slopes of the Alpe d'Huez. Pounding off the Serpentine bridge and swinging on to the towpath, some of the riders almost brushed the barriers on the outside of the right-hand bend.

If you wanted to get an idea of how fast they were going, you only needed to watch the bike-laden service cars attempting to keep up through the fast corners. Not since traffic lights were installed 20 years ago have vehicles managed such speeds around Hyde Park Corner, where the S-bend was tricky enough to unseat the Australian sprinter Stuart O'Grady, who was on his way to a fast time but eventually finished 179th.

Vladimir Gusev of Russia set the benchmark with a time of 9min 15sec, and an hour later Andreas Klöden came along to beat it by 12sec. That set off a furious battle in which the German's time was unsuccessfully attacked by his American team-mate George Hincapie and by Wiggins, who, as a child, learnt to ride a bike in Hyde Park but was ultimately to fall short of achieving the ambition of a home victory. Of the other British riders, Millar finished 13th, Geraint Thomas 45th, Mark Cavendish 69th and Charly Wegelius 91st.

Only three competitors were left to go when Fabian Cancellara, wearing the rainbow jersey of the current world time-trial champion, rolled off the starting ramp. Straight away the Swiss rider hit a high tempo, and as he rocketed down Constitution Hill he was turning his big gear so fast that he almost caught his startled motorcycle escorts, who were forced to accelerate away. When the clock stopped on a time of 8:50.74, faster than Klöden by 13sec, there were gasps from those watching the big screens around the course, followed by a half-minute of sustained applause.

So *merci*, Henri Desgrange, for inventing this unique institution, and thank you, Ken Livingstone, for bringing it to London more than a century later. As the crowds drifted away in a golden haze at the end of a perfect day, it was almost enough to earn the mayor forgiveness for those bendy buses that so regularly endanger the lives of London's bicycle commuters. Almost, but not quite.

CHEATING AND SPORT: THE FRENCH VIEW

Plus ça change ... they started cheating in 1904
by Francois Thomazeau
The Observer, 29 July 2007

The nearest the Tour de France came to being permanently cancelled was in 1904 – its second year of existence. Some riders took the train while others hitch-hiked. The editor of sports daily *L'Auto*, ancestor of today's *L'Équipe*, was forced to disqualify the four leading riders in the overall standings, handing victory to 20-year-old Henri Cornet.

The race's founder, would-be press baron Henri Desgrange, was so appalled he nearly threw in the towel, but gave the Tour one last chance. The reprieve went on for another century, turning a mere cycling race into an icon of French culture and a piece of national heritage that only world wars have managed to halt.

The competition came full circle this year, turning back to its roots to kick out race leader Michael Rasmussen. The Dane's expulsion would not have been such a blow if American Floyd Landis, who raised his arms in victory on the Champs-Élysées last summer, had not failed a dope test soon afterwards for testosterone. That meant the Tour left London without the famous yellow jersey awarded to the winner.

Even doping is not a recent Tour fixture. In 1924, French darlings the Pélissier brothers quit the race in the Normandy town of Coutances, summoned the press to a café and opened their bags to show the pills the demands of the Tour forced them to swallow – strychnine, cocaine and other unidentified stimulants. But fans were far more shocked by the withdrawal of Henri Pélissier, the 1923 winner and France's most popular sportsman at the time, than by the contents of his bag.

Plus ça change. French riders sat down before the start of what should have been the highlight stage of the 2007 Tour in the Pyrenees to protest after it was revealed that Alexander Vinokourov, seen by many best placed to claim Lance Armstrong's heritage, was a cheat. The Kazakh's only claim now is for the best quote of this Tour: "To believe I received a blood transfusion from my father is nonsense. If that was the case, I would have failed a dope test for vodka."

Should the Tour have been stopped in 1904? Should it be stopped now? A century ago, *L'Auto*'s competitors seized the opportunity to attack it as a joke. These days, French quality papers have repeatedly asked for the Tour to be stopped. The calls grew louder after the 1998 scandal, which revealed the widespread use of EPO, a growth hormone, by the Festina team.

While those who never had any interest in it ask for the Tour to stop, crowds keep lining French roads hoping to catch a glimpse of the most talked-about event of the summer. TV audiences are increasing – perhaps, ironically, because of the doping scandals. It was estimated that two million watched the start in London.

As decor, Le Tour has not lost its prestige; only its casting is wrong. Rasmussen's dominance on the mountains was so suspicious, at times grotesque, that his final victory would have been like a porn movie winning the Palme d'Or at the Cannes Film Festival. While his expulsion finally turned the Tour into a *film noir*, victory by Alberto Contador, the 24-year-old Spaniard, though not ideal, was not so tough to accept. As an Italian colleague put it: "Do you destroy La Scala because the tenor sings out of tune?"

Those wishing for the Tour to die seem to hanker after a golden age when cyclists were healthy young men competing in a gentlemanly and drug-free competition. Unfortunately, the Tour never was such an ideal world.

Francois Thomazeau is a sportswriter with Le Monde.

CHEMICALS, PAINKILLERS AND FLATULENCE: MY LIFE AS AN AMATEUR CYCLIST

by Peter Walker

The Guardian, 17 July 2008

As this year's Tour de France has again highlighted, a depressing number of professional cyclists take to the roads with the contents of a small pharmacy coursing through their veins. Every season it's the same: promises of a cleaner, brighter Tour ... followed by a slew of positive tests, usually for the blood-boosting drug EPO.

But what many don't realise – and I only appreciated very recently – is that even the most squeaky clean of riders spend much of their careers, in full concordance with the rules, stuffing themselves with a bewildering array of chemicals and potions.

Last year I took part in what was, for a bumbling amateur like myself, about as close to the Tour de France lifestyle as I could expect to experience: the Trans-Alp, an eight-day mountain bike race through the hiking paths and dirt roads of southern Germany, Austria and Italy.

While the professionals at the head of the field dashed through each stage in around three or four hours, those of us near the back spent around twice that time in the saddle every day.

This raised an inevitable question: with a leisurely lunch, even for those aiming simply not to finish last, out of the question, how do you fuel your body through a day of punishing exercise? The answer is the murky – not to mention additive-heavy – world of energy gels and drink mixes.

After months of healthy eating in preparation for the race, the moment stage one began I began an apparent mission to cram as many e-numbers and artificial flavourings into my system as possible. My daily regime was based around litres of drink powder, designed to both replace salts lost by sweating and provide carbohydrate energy. Allegedly "citrus" flavour, it tasted like someone had semi-dissolved several spoonfuls of instant mashed potato into pond water.

Augmenting this were the energy gels, small sachets of sickly-sweet chemical gunk loaded with enough sugars that if you gave one to a child they wouldn't sleep for a month. Held in reserve for the most difficult climbs were the heavily caffeinated variants, so powerful they could quite conceivably be sold to teenagers as a party drug.

Then came the energy bars, which ranged from almost healthy mixes of oats and dried fruit to day-glo pink sticks of solid Plasticine. Finally, as a chaser, came innumerable heavy-duty painkillers to numb the sore backs and aching buttocks. The jokes soon began about "Team Robert Downey Jr".

A few days into this diet and my teeth were furred, my taste buds dulled and my stomach rumbling furiously. These were common complaints – you soon learned not to cycle too closely behind fellow members of an increasingly flatulent peleton.

But this, remember, was little more than a week. Aside from a three-week Tour de France and other stage races, top road riders spend months grinding out hours of training miles fuelled by similar substances. How do they do it? I have no idea. But I also wouldn't be surprised if, on occasions, a quick shot of testosterone or some extra red blood cells actually feels like the healthy option.

CAVENDISH BRUSHES OFF LOCAL DIFFICULTY AS HE MATCHES BRITISH RECORD

The French have trouble with the sprinter's tongue but his talent is undisputed, by Richard Williams
The Guardian, 16 July 2009

After another withering victory in a bunch sprint at the end of yesterday's 11th stage of the Tour de France, with which he regained the points leader's green jersey and equalled a British record, Mark Cavendish found himself being called to account over allegations that he has been displaying signs of arrogance.

Accused by *L'Équipe*, the French sports daily newspaper, of uttering lurid anti-French remarks while being kept in a queue at an airport on Sunday night, he provided a response quite as entertaining as the race itself.

"I think I get hot-headed sometimes," he said. "I got shown the article this morning. It might have been nice to have the name of the writer of the article or the name of the rider who's supposedly said these things, so that I could go and see what the problem was. I take it as a compliment that they're going to try and start shit about something that's nothing to do with my bike riding, because they've got nothing to criticise my bike riding about. I made an effort this winter to try and learn French. I'm not confident enough yet to talk it, but I can understand questions. I love to come here and race. For sure I'm going to get arsey at some riders, because I'm an asshole, but their nationality is irrelevant. I've got to laugh at it and brush it off. But the damage is done now. Half of France got up this morning and read it."

Cavendish also swept aside an accusation that, while riding with the *autobus* – the group of sprinters at the rear of the field – during Saturday's mountain stage, he failed to do his share of work to maintain the pace. "I'm in a good team and I've got to save my energy," he said. "Maybe it's because there are no doping stories and they've got to find something to write about."

There is something of the scally – of the young Wayne Rooney, even – in the way the 24-year-old from the Isle of Man tends to get his punch in first and apologise, if absolutely necessary, later. A volatile nature is useful to a sprinter, who is required to explode off the front of a bunch and take no prisoners in the final metres, but the rough edge of Cavendish's tongue, amusing as it can be, will require smoothing away sooner or later.

Yesterday, having equalled Barry Hoban's record of eight stage wins in the Tour, set between 1967 and 1975, he almost slipped again when asked if he had discussed the sprinter's art with the Yorkshireman.

"Yes." A pause. "He's a nice guy." Another pause. "He talks a lot to me a dinners and so on, and he's given me some advice, but he's also said some things in the press that offended me a little bit." A longer pause. "But it's nice to be able to be spoken of in the same sentence as one of the great British sprinters."

An hour earlier there had been nothing but sure-footedness in the way Cavendish's Columbia-HTC team set him up for the final dash to the line. He had watched the overhead footage of the previous day's sprint and noted how it looked like "a fruit salad of team colours", with the white line of the nine Columbia riders down the middle, maintaining perfect discipline. "That's how it was again today," he said, pointing out that it was not a team custom-built for the sole purpose of catapulting him to the finish. "There's Kim Kirchen, who's a massive contender for the general classification, there's Maxime Monfort, who's a climber, there's Bert Grabsch, the world time-trial champion, and there's Mick Rogers, also a time trial champion. They all know that if they commit themselves 100 per cent then we've got the best chance of coming out victorious, and they'll ride for that."

With 150 metres to go he was about to take the lead from Mark Renshaw, the last of his lead-out men, when Thor Hushovd appeared at his shoulder. The sight of the green jersey, taken from him by the Norwegian in Barcelona last Thursday, was enough to inspire a final blast that took him to the line, with the American rider Tyler Farrar in second place, Yauheni Hutarovich of Belarus in third and Hushovd fading to fifth.

There was good news at the start of the day for Bradley Wiggins, one of 100 riders given a time 15 seconds slower than that of the 52 leaders in Issoudun on Tuesday after the *peloton* had been split by a crash a few hundred metres from the finish line. Eventually the judges ruled all the riders could be given the same time, and Wiggins was able to start and finish yesterday's stage restored to fifth place in the overall standings. The holders of the yellow and polka-dot jerseys, Rinaldo Nocentini of Italy and Egoi Martínez of Spain, remain unchanged.

Today's flattish stage from Tonnerre to Vittel is likely to offer Cavendish the chance to erase Hoban's record, and perhaps to undergo another test of his diplomatic skills.

MARK CAVENDISH SPRINTS TO VICTORY ON CHAMPS-ÉLYSÉES

by Jeremy Campbell
The Guardian, 26 July 2009

Mark Cavendish won the final stage of the Tour de France with another magnificent sprint, beating his nearest rival by over 30 metres at the famous finish on the Champs-Élysées in Paris. It takes his stage wins for this year's Tour to six and his tally overall to 10. Last week he had eclipsed Barry Hoban's record for a British rider of eight and it is only the 24-year-old's second Tour.

INTERVIEW – BRADLEY WIGGINS: "I ATTACKED ARMSTRONG AND HAD AN OUT-OF-BODY EXPERIENCE"

British rider says he can win the Tour de France after a spiritual date with Simpson on the road to fourth place, by Donald McRae

The Guardian, 4 August 2009

Bradley Wiggins, hunched in a chair and speaking quietly through his exhaustion, remembers the suffering during his hardest day on the Tour de France. It is a chilling moment. He has already revealed that he sometimes thinks of himself as a "fraud" for finishing fourth in the race, despite his compelling courage and resilience, and in a contrasting statement has said that he plans eventually to win the Tour. But this is different.

This is a downbeat murmur that causes goosebumps to rise. For a second Wiggins looks as though he has seen the ghost of Tom Simpson again, the haunting British cyclist who died on the slopes of Mont Ventoux during the 1967 Tour de France.

"I don't want this to sound cheesy," Wiggins says, fearing that a surreal experience might be misconstrued as the delusions of a man driven mad after 2,200 miles on his bike. "But when I reached Ventoux on the second-last day it felt as if Tom was waiting for me. As I began the climb it felt as if his spirit was riding with me. It started on the early slopes and I imagined how Tom must have been feeling, riding towards his death, and the feeling grew as I climbed.

"There were times when Andy Schleck [who finished second behind Alberto Contador, and just ahead of Lance Armstrong and Wiggins] was attacking and it was horrible. I thought, 'I can't go on. I can't do this anymore …' But I then thought more vividly of Tom and how he must have felt that last day. It was like a reason not to give up. I felt like I was doing it more for his memory than anything."

Wiggins pauses, ducking his head shyly, as if he might have gone too far. But the 29-year-old, who has turned himself from a three-times Olympic gold medal-winning track pursuit rider into one of the world's great road cyclists, smiles wryly when I stretch out my arms to show him the sudden gooseflesh.

"That's the feeling I had," he says. "A lot of riders will take the piss out of me for saying this – but I don't think they fully respect the history of the race. A lot of young riders in the *peloton* think they're 'it' at 22. And I'm not referring to Mark Cavendish [the British sprinter who won an extraordinary six stages of the Tour] in any way. But half the *peloton* don't even know that a person, Tom Simpson, died on the Ventoux. That's terribly sad."

THE TOUR DE FRANCE

Carrying a small photograph of Simpson with him, to steel himself for a climb that he feared might break him after three weeks on the road, Wiggins was aware that "90 per cent of them rode slowly up the Ventoux, chatting to each other, knowing their race was over. It was different up front. We had to hit it hard – because the next few hours would decide where we ended on the Tour. I was exhausted, and emotional, but there were times when I felt fantastic."

Just as Simpson's drug-streaked death was a tangled affair, Wiggins's intense emotions are complicated. "It's difficult to describe because I feel a bit of a fraud in some aspects. Tom Simpson is like the Bobby Moore of British cycling. I wouldn't say he was a hero of mine because he was dead a long time before I was born. But I hold him in such high esteem. So it doesn't feel real. Great names finish up there in the Tour. People like [Carlos] Sastre ..."

The Spanish winner of the 2008 Tour finished 13 places behind Wiggins this year. And yet, as I remind him, Wiggins outclimbed Sastre and Cadel Evans. "Yeah," he grins, "and [Andreas] Klöden [a former Tour runner-up who finished sixth]. I beat all those guys. The first time I realised I could do it was on Verbier [on the middle Sunday]. I attacked Armstrong's group and I had an out-of-body experience there – where I saw myself leaving Klöden, Evans and

Armstrong in the Tour de bloody France. It didn't feel right. It was very strange."

He laughs quietly – but it's a rasping half-laugh, half-cough. It echoes again later when we walk through central London, and Wiggins talks about feeling so poorly, with his depleted body no longer able to fight the sniffles, sore throat and muscle-eating fatigue that followed his drastic weight-loss and ravaged immune system. He shed 20 pounds before the Tour started so that he could swap his power on the track for a skeletal lightness in the mountains. It is just one consequence of his epic tilt at sporting greatness. "I've been running at 4 per cent body fat the last few weeks – and that's quite dangerous. I'm starting to get sick now, a little ill, just from being run down. I'm just glad I'm now free to put a few pounds back on."

Wiggins is aware of the irony that Simpson rode Ventoux the last time on amphetamines, chased down by brandy, with the drugs costing him his life. "I'm sure there were also a few grumbles about me, and suspicions, because I've come from nowhere. That's partly why I released my blood tests for the past two years last week. The evidence is there for people to see. My attitude is that if you have nothing to hide why not show it?"

The Tour's doping history is so grim that misgivings about others remain. Do the *peloton* have doubts in regard to Contador – who proved himself to be on a different level from every other rider in both the mountains and the time-trial? "I don't think so. I didn't hear any mention of doping on the whole Tour – which is amazing. I'm just hoping we don't get any drug revelations over the next few weeks."

Yet Greg LeMond, a former three-times winner of the Tour, suggests that Contador's VO2 max (his body's ability to absorb and use oxygen) must exceed that of any other athlete who has ever lived. "The burden is on Contador to prove he is physically capable of performing this feat without performance-enhancing products," LeMond argues. Contador's supporters retort that LeMond bases his measurement of VO2 max on flawed data, which fails to take altitude into account.

"I don't know much about any of that stuff," Wiggins says, shrugging. "I just know Contador's going to be the man to beat for the next five years. I don't think there was a big divide between me and Frank Schleck [who finished fifth] and Lance. There is a gap between me and Contador that will be harder to close. But who knows how far I can go? Coming into this Tour I thought privately that I could make the top 10 – and my only doubt was on the mental side. I thought I would crack first mentally, rather than physically. But it's different now.

"Winning the Tour has to be my goal now. I would never say, 'OK, this is my goal: to finish third.' My goal is to win the race. Logically, I've got to be in with a real shot. I was a definite contender this year and I'm only going to get better. And Lance is only going to get older …"

The throaty cackle comes again – and Wiggins checks himself briefly. "But Lance is the only bike rider I've ever met who has that aura. He's like no one else. But we got on fine because I treat him like a normal person. It was different between him and [Armstrong's team-mate] Contador. It got to the point where I wouldn't have been surprised if they got off their bikes and ended up fighting each other. Everyone knew there was bad blood and it looks like, reading the war on Twitter between them, it's not yet over."

Armstrong is likely to be interested in Cavendish and Wiggins when he finally retires and concentrates on building his own team. If Cavendish speaks of his awe for Armstrong, Wiggins is more measured. "It would be interesting to ride for someone like Lance but Andy Schleck is going there. And after this Tour I've reached the point where I need to be the leader. I've gone up to another level – of Tour contender status – and once people wave chequebooks at you it changes a lot. I'm quite happy where I am and I've had success here. But we'll see what happens once my contract [with Garmin-Slipstream] ends next year."

The determination of Dave Brailsford and the British Sky team to entice Wiggins away from Garmin – if not next year then certainly in 2011 – clearly intrigues him. He praises his current team-mates, especially the previous leader, Christian Vande Velde, who stepped down to support Wiggins, but his relationship with British cycling is so strong that it is hard to imagine him not joining Sky.

"That idea definitely appeals to me. I'd like to ride the Tour one day with a British team. It would be like the track – no detail will be missed. The Tour is all about detail and this year, because I didn't expect to be in my position, we didn't recce the course or study the climbs."

The prospect of Wiggins working with meticulous coaches such as Brailsford and Shane Sutton on future Tours – and fulfilling predictions of a British winner – might be made still more fascinating should Cavendish eventually complete the dream package. "We did something special this year, me and Cav," Wiggins says. "He said he was very proud of me and likewise me of him. Six stage wins is phenomenal – and he's now won 10 in two years. We're on to something incredible with British cycling. We've done it on the track but the medals we won in Beijing felt almost business-like – because it was so expected. The Tour was more magical."

CHAPTER EIGHT
INTO THE FUTURE

Start 3 July
Rotterdam

NETHERLANDS

Finish 25 July
Paris Champs-Elysees

BELGIUM

Arenberg Porte
du Hainaut

Brussels

Reims
Epernay

Spa

Longjumeau

Cambrai

Wanze

BELGIUM

Finish
Paris

Reims
Epernay

FRANCE

Montargis

FRANCE

Bourg-de-Peage

Pauillac

Tournus

Bordeaux

Mende

Rodez

Bourg-les-
Valence

Sisteron

Gueugnon

Station des Rousses

Morzine-Avoriaz

Chambery

Salies-de-Bearn

Pau

Pamiers

Revel

Saint-Jean-de-Maurienne

Gap

Col du Tourmalet

Ax-3 Domaines

Sisteron

Bagneres-de-Luchon

100 MILES

Stage start   Stage start / finish   Stage finish   Rest day   Individual time-trial   Prologue

LEADERS HEAD INTO THE CIRCLE OF DEATH, WHERE THE TOUR CELEBRATES A CENTURY OF SUFFERING

The race organisers were labelled "assassins" 100 years ago but today is Schleck's turn to take aim, by Richard Williams

22 July 2010

When Alberto Contador and Andy Schleck fight for victory in the 2010 Tour de France on the pitiless slopes of the Col du Tourmalet this afternoon, they will be accompanied by the words of Henri Desgrange as he surveyed the success of his decision, exactly 100 years ago, to add stages in the high mountains to his great invention. "The Tour de France only became the Tour de France," the founder said, "when we sent the riders into the mountains."

The Tourmalet was the first of those mountains, inserted into the eighth edition of the race in 1910 after Alphonse Steines, Desgrange's assistant, had reconnoitered the route the previous year. Discovering an unmade road rendered impassable by snow, Steines dismissed his driver and continued on foot. He got lost, fell down a ravine and had to be rescued, but the following morning, in a gendarmerie in the hamlet of Bareges on the way down from the 2,115m summit, he cabled his boss: "Tourmalet crossed stop very good road stop perfectly practicable stop Steines."

Whether or not they know his name, generations of riders have had reason both to bless and to curse the assistant race director's judgment. The first to register his opinion, when the race went over the pass on July 21 1910, was Octave Lapize, who was seen to be walking alongside his heavy single-speed bike in a state of some distress. The next man to arrive, half an hour later, was Gustave Garrigou, who had actually managed to ride his machine up the final gradient.

As Lapize crossed the summit of the next pass, the Col d'Aubisque, he hurled a famous imprecation at the commissaires. "You are all assassins," he shouted with what remained of his strength. "No human being should be put through an ordeal like this. That's enough for me." Nevertheless he carried on, thereby establishing a precedent for an ineluctable combination of cyclists, mountains and suffering. Having set off from Luchon, the riders had already covered 140km, and still had 150km to go to the finish in Bayonne. Ten days later Lapize was celebrating victory in Paris, with Garrigou second, having covered a route of 4,737km in 31 days.

Today's riders enjoy the benefits of asphalted roads, carbon-fibre bikes weighing a fraction of the contraptions of a century ago, scientifically developed fitness programmes and diets (in 1910 the defending champion, Francois Faber, set off into the Pyrenees with 12 veal cutlets in his bag, saying, "It's because I eat like four men that I can fight against five"). Today's stage measures a mere 174km, which they will cover in around five hours.

In many respects, life is far easier for them. Three years after Lapize's pioneering ascent, Eugène Christophe was on the slopes of the Tourmalet when a collision with a car broke his front fork. After pushing the damaged bike 15km to Sainte Marie de Campan, he used the village smithy to mend the break. But the regulations of those days sternly stipulated that the riders had to do all the work on their bikes themselves, and Christophe had enlisted the aid of a boy to operate the forge's bellows while he made the repair. His 10-minute penalty added to the four hours he had lost ended his hopes of victory. Nowadays team vehicles are at hand to provide a new bike within seconds of a problem occurring, while some adjustments can be made on the move, by mechanics leaning out of the car to wield an Allen key. The faces of this year's riders, however, have demonstrated that the suffering persists.

Some riders, a select few, have made light of the Tourmalet's challenge. The great Spanish climber Federico Bahamontes, forever known as the Eagle of Toledo, led over the summit on four occasions, and in 1954 he even stopped for an ice cream to let the others catch up and accompany him on the descent, a skill at which he was less adept.

The Pyrenees, of which the Tourmalet is the great symbol in the race's iconography, may not be as familiar to casual enthusiasts as the Alps, but they are riddled with memories of heroism. Many connoisseurs relish the way they present the riders with one challenge after another, testing the final reserves of spirit and courage. Not for nothing are the mountains around the Tourmalet known as the Circle of Death.

In 1947 Jean Robic, the bad-tempered Frenchman who sported an unstylish leather crash helmet, rode alone across four of the cols, including the Tourmalet, to capture the stage from Luchon to Pau, later snatching victory on the final day and winning the Tour without ever wearing the leader's yellow jersey. Two years later the stage was reversed and Robic won again, although two Italians were depicted that day in one of cycling's most indelible images, when a photographer captured Fausto Coppi sharing his water bottle with Gino Bartali, his greatest rival, on a blisteringly hot day.

It was in 1969 that Eddy Merckx led the way up the Tourmalet with a group including Roger Pingeon and Raymond Poulidor, en route to winning the first of his five Tours. Just below the summit he attacked and rode alone for

140km to reach the stage finish in Mourenx eight minutes ahead of his pursuers.

Before this year's riders even reach the Tourmalet they will have to tackle the Col de Marie-Blanque, barely half its big brother's stature but offering almost 10km of gradients that average a punishing 9 per cent. "A tense, cheerless climb" is how Graeme Fife describes it in his fine volume, *The Great Road Climbs of the Pyrenees.* And then, to stretch the aching legs still further, and perhaps to sow further doubts, comes the 1,474m Col du Soulor, with a plunging, twisting descent – particularly dangerous if the predicted rain arrives – before the riders gather themselves for the final major climb of this year's Tour, and a mountain-top finish that may have a decisive effect on the final standings in Paris on Sunday.

As Contador and Schleck soar up to play among peaks where birds of prey wheel on the thermals, which of them will be the eagle and which the vulture? Having been let down by his machinery in the very act of attacking on the other side of the Tourmalet on Tuesday, the boyish Luxembourgeois knows this is his last chance to claw back an eight-second deficit and open up the lead of three minutes or so that would make it hard for the Spaniard to exploit his known superiority in Saturday's 52km time trial.

Schleck may go for an early attack on the Marie-Blanque or the Soulor, although Contador's Astana lieutenants – notably Alexander Vinokourov, Daniel Navarro and Paolo Tiralongo – appear well capable of guarding the yellow jersey's interests and neutralising a concerted effort from the Saxo Bank boys. More likely Schleck will hope to burn Contador off his wheel with a solo break on the lower slopes of the Tourmalet. Success would not guarantee him the glory on the Champs-Élysées, but it would give this Tour its most powerful moment as well as paying the finest of birthday tributes to a mountain whose brutal demands have shaped history.

HATRED NEEDED TO KEEP WHEELS IN MOTION

Respect between riders goes against the grain of true Tour de France rivalry, writes Richard Williams
The Guardian, 27 July 2010

After all the smiles and handshakes, it was surprising that Alberto Contador and Andy Schleck didn't blow kisses to each other as they stood on the podium in Paris on Sunday evening. We can only hope that beneath their avowals of respect and friendship lurk the elements of a true Tour de France rivalry: simmering resentment and something close to hatred.

Since their battle over the three weeks of the 2010 Tour concluded with a repeat of the previous year's result, and it seems more than likely that there will be more to come next year, there needs to be something more than sun-kissed displays of magnanimous sporting behaviour if this historic race is to maintain its vibrancy.

A "clean" Tour in terms of dope tests is one thing (although we must wait for a month or two before being entirely comfortable about that assertion). Extending it to the competition between the riders is quite another.

"What we've seen between the two favourites is inconceivable," the two-times winner Laurent Fignon, who knows a thing or two about bitter personal rivalries, said on the eve of the final stage. "Cycling isn't a friendly game. The competition should be pitiless. When you're rivals, you can't love each other. In fact you mustn't love each other."

During the winner's press conference, which traditionally takes place the night before the ride into Paris, Contador suddenly put Schleck in his place. He started silkily enough. "Andy is a great rider," he said. "I've spent a lot of time with him. I know the way he works and I think he's going to be a major rival for a long time. He's very young, and I'm still very young, and I'm sure he's going to keep improving." Then he inserted the stiletto. "He was at the same level this year. I wasn't. We'll see what happens in the future."

Contador said that he had been taking antibiotics before the Tour started and that he was in a bad way the night before Saturday's 52km time trial, in which he performed way below the standard he exhibited in winning the equivalent stage in Annecy last year, when he beat even Fabian Cancellara over a 40km course.

If the subtext of Contador's remarks is to be taken seriously, Schleck's success in closing the margin between them from 4min 11sec in 2009 to 39sec this year is no more than an illusion, and not to be taken as an indication that the Luxembourg rider is on the brink of overhauling the Spaniard.

Contador is probably right, and the key to this particular ascendancy is surely Schleck's inability to go off on long-range attacks in the high mountains. His repeated short bursts again had no lasting impact, and he will have to expand his range of weaponry if he hopes to do anything other than wait for Contador to retire before claiming his first yellow jersey in Paris. He has shown signs of raising his game in the time trials, so there may be hope.

Should he fail to take the final step, the world will be looking for other young contenders as the generation of Carlos Sastre, Ivan Basso, Cadel Evans and Bradley Wiggins starts to

fade away. Sky's Edvald Boasson Hagen is an obvious candidate, although the 23-year-old Norwegian all-rounder, the
winner of last year's Tour of Britain, was badly hampered by
bronchitis in his first Tour de France, finishing two consecutive mountain stages alongside the sprinters in the *grupetto*.

Others include the riders in fifth, sixth and seventh places
in this year's final general classification: Jurgen Van den
Broeck, Omega Pharma-Lotto's 27-year-old Belgian; Robert
Gesink, Rabobank's 24-year-old Dutchman; and Ryder
Hesjedal of Garmin-Transitions.

Will Ben Swift or Peter Kennaugh emerge from the ranks
of Team Sky's juniors with the qualities to challenge one day
for the overall win? On their young shoulders, at the moment,
rests the burden of Dave Brailsford's much-publicised intention to put a British rider on the top step of the podium.

Even when the rivalries are coated with honey, the world
of the Tour de France is a harsh one. That's the way it was
meant to be, and anything else would be an insult to those
who fought the grim battles of yesteryear.

OBITUARY: LAURENT FIGNON

Champion French cyclist best known for his epic defeat in the 1989 Tour de France, by William Fotheringham

The Guardian, 2 September 2010

Laurent Fignon, who has died of cancer aged 50, won the Tour de France twice, but was also widely celebrated for losing it, in the narrowest defeat in Tour history. He was a charismatic cycling champion with trenchant views on his sport, the last Frenchman who seemed capable of living up to national expectations in the Tour, which he dominated with such insouciant ease in 1984 that the cycling magazine *Vélo* published his photograph that July along with a one-word caption: *l'Ogre.*

Nicknamed "the professor" after an abortive attempt at university studies, and with distinctive looks – long blond hair, thick-lensed spectacles and a John McEnroe-style headband – the Paris-born Fignon had the cycling world briefly at his feet after winning five stages in his Renault team's total of 10 (out of a possible 23), at the age of 23. His fellow Frenchman Bernard Hinault, who had dominated cycling for six years, finished more than 10 minutes behind, and had never looked Fignon's physical equal. On one occasion, Fignon was asked how he felt when Hinault attacked. His answer was: "When I saw him going up the road, I had to laugh."

The dominance was brief, although the expectations survived a little longer. Fignon's place in cycling history is based on the celebrated role he played as the runner-up in the greatest Tour ever, in 1989. By then he had spent four years trying to regain his best level after two achilles tendon operations in 1985. His battle with the American Greg LeMond was a tense affair, with the two men swapping the lead for the three-week duration of the race until Fignon carved out a 50-second lead before the final stage, a time trial into Paris.

Fignon felt his advantage was sufficient, but he was suffering from an abscess which made it virtually impossible for him to sit on his bike, and LeMond was using radical new aerodynamic handlebars. Fignon crossed the line on the Champs-Élysées and subsided in tears on the cobbles, having lost by just eight seconds after almost 88 hours of racing – still the narrowest margin in Tour history. It was a brutal defeat, a magnificent comeback for LeMond – who had come close to death in a shooting accident the previous year – and its impact turned the Tour into a truly global sports event.

Fignon won other major races – the Milan–San Remo Classic in 1988 and 1989, the Giro d'Italia in 1989 – and suffered a controversial defeat in the Giro in 1984, when the organisers pulled out all the stops to ensure a home victory. But his impact extended beyond his victories and his great defeat. In 1985, when Renault pulled out of sponsorship, he and his manager, Cyrille Guimard, came up with a novel system of managing team finances. Previously, teams had tended to belong to the sponsor, and were vulnerable when a backer lost interest. Instead, Guimard and Fignon set up their own company to run the team and own its assets, selling advertising space on the team's jerseys and cars to a main sponsor. Most professional cycling teams are run in this way today.

He was also one of few cyclists to reinvest their winnings in their sport. After retirement in 1993, he set up a promotions company to run events for cycle tourists, and he bought the second-biggest race in French cycling, the Paris–Nice "race to the sun", in 2000. As an organiser, he was unable to compete with the Amaury Sport Organisation, which has a virtual monopoly on major races in France, including the Tour, and he eventually sold Paris–Nice to them in 2002.

Subsequently he scaled down his promotional ventures and put his energy into developing a training centre in the Pyrenees. He also published his memoirs, *Nous Etions Jeunes et Insouciants* (2009), which I translated into English this summer under the title *We Were Young and Carefree*. The book was painfully honest about his attempts to get back to full fitness after his operations, spoke mercilessly about former rivals and described an epic drinking session with Hinault and an occasion on which Fignon lied to his manager to enable a team-mate to use his hotel room for a romantic assignation with "an unofficial Miss France".

Fignon's main premise was that cycling was "a living, breathing art", a world that created "complete men rather than just sportsmen", and that it had been robbed of much of its magic by the demands of sponsors and the widespread use of the blood-boosting drug erythropoietin, which he contrasted with his own amateurish use of cortisone and amphetamine.

He worked as a television commentator on the 2009 and 2010 Tours, in spite of his illness – the harsh croak of his voice will remain my enduring memory of this year's race – and in one of his last interviews, in January, he was typically forthright about his health: "I don't want to die at 50, but if there is no cure, what can I do? I'm not afraid of dying. I just don't want it to happen."

He is survived by his second wife, Valerie, and by a son, Jeremy, and a daughter, Tiphaine, from his first marriage.

Laurent Patrick Fignon, cyclist, born August 12 1960; died August 31 2010

REVIEW: RACING THROUGH THE DARK BY DAVID MILLAR, ORION

by Richard Williams

The Guardian, 18 June 2011

Within the space of 24 hours last month, professional bike racers forced the cancellation of a stage of the Tour of California because of cold weather and persuaded the organisers of the Giro d'Italia to bypass a particularly dangerous descent. A reader of Richard Moore's *Slaying the Badger*, an account of the ferocious battle between Bernard Hinault and Greg LeMond for supremacy in the 1986 Tour de France, might come across the tale of Hinault – the Badger of the title – suffering severe frostbite while riding to victory through snow and ice early in his career and conclude that today's riders have gone soft.

If that reader were then to encounter David Millar's harrowing description of his mental and physical ordeal on an Alpine stage of the 2010 Tour de France, which forms the climax of *Racing Through the Dark*, a different impression might be entertained. Millar's suffering that day is the sort of thing that forms an unbreakable link between cycling's rich history and its present.

By the time we reach his Calvary on the Col de la Madeleine, we have travelled with Millar from his origins as a party-loving expat brat in Hong Kong to his current status as one of the world's leading riders, via the life-changing consequences of the single most dramatic incident of his career: the night in 2001 when two French policemen led him out of a restaurant in Biarritz, his adopted home, and, with the aid of two empty syringes found in his apartment, induced him to confess to having used illegal performance-enhancing drugs in order to achieve some of his greatest triumphs.

Some, but not all. When he was 23 years old and still drug-free, Millar won an important stage of the Tour de France. Drugs alone did not make him a top rider. Gradually, however, this intelligent, articulate, emotionally volatile, intellectually inquisitive young man, who would have gone to art college had he not become a professional racer, allowed himself to be sucked into the culture of doping.

Like many others, he had grown frustrated by being part of a *peloton à deux vitesses*, in which the doped riders almost invariably beat their clean rivals with demoralising ease. There was a natural progression from regular "recovery" injections of vitamins through the use of cortisone to the quasi-scientific administering of EPO, a hormone boosting the production of red blood cells. This changed the doping game in the 1990s, when riders moved beyond crude stimulants such as the notorious "*pot Belge*", a concoction of amphetamine and heroin, to substances that increased their capacity for physical endurance to inhuman levels.

Millar's description of his fall is laceratingly honest, detailing every twist in the argument by which he convinced himself to take a step he had previously considered unthinkable. Most of the men who helped him to destroy himself, either by supplying substances, sharing their expertise or turning a blind eye, are named, but that is not really the point: anyone seeking to understand the motivation of a drug cheat, or wondering why such a man should be allowed back into his sport after serving his two-year suspension, will find their curiosity satisfied here.

Since returning to competition in 2006, Millar has taken every opportunity to campaign against doping, speaking eloquently from a position of considerable authority. He lost the thread of his career and is now determined to help save his sport by preventing others from falling into the same trap. Cyclists still dope, but a smaller proportion than 10 years ago and with a greater chance of getting caught.

This is an urgent tale, told in an authentic voice. His portraits of contemporaries such as Bradley Wiggins and Mark Cavendish are vividly intimate and shrewdly observed. The recollection of his meeting with Lance Armstrong at the end of the 2007 tour, when he accused the man who had been among his early supporters of abusing the sport, is chilling. And the description of that agonising mountain stage last summer, during which he scoured the depths of his soul while falling helplessly behind the rest of the field, deserves to stand among the great first-person accounts of sporting experience.

THE GRIT THAT DROVE OLD MAN EVANS TO THE SUMMIT

by Richard Williams

The Guardian, 25 July 2011

Cadel Evans duly crossed the finish line in the yellow jersey yesterday, the first Australian winner in the history of the Tour de France. But two days earlier and at the other end of the country there had been a moment when it looked as though the game might be up for the man who had twice lost the race by less than a minute and who had gained a reputation for attracting misfortune.

When Alberto Contador suddenly attacked, barely 20km into Friday's stage and soon after the riders had begun to climb the lower ramps of the Col du Télégraphe, Andy Schleck jumped away in instinctive pursuit of the defending champion. Behind them Evans wobbled, slowed to a halt and got off his bike. He looked at his back wheel in suspicion, shook it, and then remounted, getting a push from a fat man in a replica *maillot jaune*.

His BMC team-mate Marcus Burghardt slowed in order to help him with the task of rejoining the small elite group now rapidly disappearing up the road, but a minute later Evans was off his bike again. What fresh catastrophe was this? The team car arrived and he was handed a new machine. When he restarted, it was as part of a larger group almost two minutes behind the leaders. It looked like a potentially decisive moment, the one in which Evans left Contador and the younger Schleck to fight it out for the yellow jersey, as they had in 2009 and 2010.

Evans, halfway though his 35th year, is the oldest Tour winner since the war, superseding Gino Bartali, the great Italian champion, whose two victories straddled the conflict and who was 34 years and one week old at the time of his second success in 1948. The oldest of all is Firmin Lambot, a Belgian maker of equestrian saddles, who was 36 in 1922 when he secured his second victory without winning a stage.

TOUR DE FRANCE: THRILLS, SPILLS AND BARBED WIRE

How the most exciting and accident-prone Tour de France in years was won, by Everton Gayle

The Guardian, 25 July 2011

STAGE 1

Crashes galore make for a nervous start in which Alberto Contador, Andy Schleck and Bradley Wiggins lose more than a minute. Philippe Gilbert outfoxes rivals to win yellow, green and polka dot jersey.

STAGE 2

Garmin-Cervelo win the team time trial, which propels Thor Hushovd into yellow.

STAGE 3

Tyler Farrar dedicates his first stage win to Wouter Weylandt, who died in the Giro.

STAGE 4

Race finishes on a climb called 'the Breton Alpe d'Huez'. Contador attacks but Cadel Evans holds him off for stage win and polka dot jersey. Hushovd is in yellow and José Joaquín Rojas wears green jersey.

STAGE 5

Wiggins crashes out of the tour while Mark Cavendish announces his arrival by turning on the power and outsprinting Gilbert and Rojas for first stage in this tour and 16th in total. Gilbert is points leader.

STAGE 6

Edvald Boasson Hagen grabs Team Sky's first stage victory.

STAGE 7

Cavendish wins again, his second in Chateauroux, after maiden stage win in 2008. Rojas takes green.

STAGE 8

Rui Alberto Costa escapes to win stage.

STAGE 9

Alexandr Vinokourov breaks a leg in a ditch and Jurgen van den Broeck quits. TV car sends Johnny Hoogerland into a barbed wire fence. Luis León Sánchez wins stage and Thomas Voeckler is in the yellow jersey.

STAGE 10

André Greipel beats his bitter sprint rival Mark Cavendish.

STAGE 11

A day after admitting that André Greipel rode a perfect sprint, Cavendish gets his own back by marshalling team-mates to lead him to the line to record his 18th stage victory and lead the race for the points jersey.

STAGE 12

Geraint Thomas misjudges a bend on the Hourquette d'Ancizan and misses out on a prize on Col du Tourmalet. Frank Schleck makes a late attack but Samuel Sánchez gets one over contenders on first mountain stage.

STAGE 13

No miracle in Lourdes as Thor Hushovd beats Jeremy Roy.

STAGE 14

After attacks and counterattacks by Andy and Frank Schleck, Jelle Vanendert launches a raid of his own and breaks away to triumph at Plateau de Beille. But Voeckler remains the overall leader.

STAGE 15

The HTC express put their foot down and do a sterling job to help Cavendish see off his rivals for the green jersey – Rojas and Gilbert – to add Montpellier to his list of conquests. It's his fourth victory in this year's Tour.

STAGE 16
Hushovd gets the better of Edvald Boasson Hagen for second stage win and 12th overall.

STAGE 17
Boasson Hagen makes amends to win his second stage and Norway's fourth.

STAGE 18
Andy Schleck's bold attack wins stage but Voeckler keeps yellow.

STAGE 19
Contador attacks on the Col du Télégraphe and on the Col du Galibier. Spaniard eventually fades, as does Voeckler. Frenchman's team-mate Pierre Rolland wins stage and Andy Schleck is in yellow.

STAGE 20
Tony Martin wins a stunning time trial in the suburbs of Grenoble but Evans sets up certain overall victory by taking

the yellow jersey from Andy Schleck. Evans is 1min 34sec ahead with Paris looming.

Stage 21

Mark Cavendish wins the green jersey and his fifth stage.

CAVENDISH EARNS PLACE IN SPRINTING HISTORY

by William Fotheringham
The Guardian, 25 July 2011

Even before his triumphant arrival in Paris in the green jersey yesterday, Mark Cavendish had carved out an enviable niche among the ranks of the Tour's sprint greats. With 20 wins in four Tours over four years, Cavendish is already more prolific than most and more consistent than all the rest. The green jersey is merely the icing on the cake.

The only sprinter who still ranks ahead of Cavendish in terms of Tour de France stages won is André Darrigade of France, who won a total of 22, but over a far longer period, between 1953 and 1964. Darrigade also won the green jersey twice, in 1959 and 1961. Both the great man's landmark achievements are well within Cavendish's reach, although it is unlikely that the Manxman will match his impressive record of winning the race's first stage five times.

If Cavendish's record for consistency in a major Tour is remarkable, it is, however, topped by one other sprinter: the Italian Mario Cipollini. His career was centred on the Giro d'Italia, however, rather than the Tour, but it offers a vision of what Cavendish may achieve in the French race. Cipollini rode to a record 42 stage victories in the Giro d'Italia between 1989 and 2003, winning the points standings three times. Something similar in the Tour is well within Cavendish's grasp: at his present rate he would surpass Eddy Merckx's Tour record of 34 some time in 2014.

Cipollini and Cavendish's records in the Tour cannot be compared, as the "Lion King" tended to be mentally and physically tired by the time he got to the Tour. Unlike Cavendish, who speaks publicly of his love of the Tour, the Italian never actually managed to finish the race although he does hold one record: four stage wins in four days in 1999.

There are those who complain that Cavendish's behaviour is sometimes over the top, but he is good taste personified compared to Cipollini. The Italian has a healthy respect for the Manxman, and described him as "conclusively the best sprinter in the world at the moment", although – ironically for a man famed for a lavish playboy lifestyle – he added that in his view Cavendish needs to work harder.

Two men have dominated the green points jersey standings in the Tour, the German Erik Zabel who won it in successive years from 1996 to 2001 – a record six wins – and who is now an adviser to Cavendish's HTC-Highroad team, and the Irishman Sean Kelly, *maillot vert* winner four times between 1982 and 1989.

The dominance of Zabel and Kelly reflects the fact that, historically, the green jersey in the Tour has not always rewarded the best sprinter – it was also won three times by Merckx as he raced to overall victory – although the organisers have rejigged the way it is awarded this year to tip the balance back in favour of the sprint specialists. Kelly was not the fastest sprinter in the Tour by any means and nor was Zabel.

Both tended to place consistently on the flat stages behind the faster sprinters and would get a huge advantage on the hillier stages where the fast men tended to be left behind. That is Thor Hushovd's style and it is one reason he managed to win the green jersey ahead of Cavendish in 2009.

Another role model for Cavendish is the Belgian Freddy Maertens, a prolific sprinter in all three major Tours, who won five stages in both the 1976 and 1981 Tours. Maertens was a prolific winner of one-day races, as was Zabel, and this is an area which Cavendish has said he will look to in the future if his sprint speed blunts a little as the years pass.

Maertens was also twice a world road-race champion, and in the coming weeks the Manxman will turn his attention to a campaign to win the world road-race title at the end of September, while he also has his sights on next year's Olympic road race.

CASE CLOSED: ARMSTRONG'S RECORD WILL BE LEFT FOR HISTORY TO JUDGE

by Richard Williams
The Guardian, 7 February 2012

The long struggle to connect Lance Armstrong with doping finally came to an effective halt on Friday afternoon with the announcement that the federal investigation into the seven-times Tour de France winner has been abandoned after the best part of two years. It feels like the end of an era, if not the end of the connection between bike racing and illegal perfor-mance enhancers, as could be seen by yesterday's conclusion to the long-running Alberto Contador affair, in which the Spaniard was stripped of his 2010 Tour win and given a two-year ban.

But Armstrong's historic series of victories in the biggest of all bike races will stand for ever in the record books, along-side the five wins of the late Jacques Anquetil, the man who said: "You do not win the Tour de France on mineral water alone," a brusque acknowledgement of behaviour that had been accepted since the earliest days of the sport.

Half a century ago, Anquetil rode in an era when riders took all sorts of stuff, including amphetamines, cocaine and heroin, to make them go faster and increase their resistance to the pain of hauling themselves up the mountains for day after day. History accepts those circumstances, to the extent that no one would wish to see the record books retrospectively altered to expunge the records of men who are regarded as heroes of a more romantic age. It could be that Armstrong, who competed at a time when the use of steroids and human growth hormone and the technique of blood doping were at their most widespread, may become the subject of a similar moral amnesty in the mind of future generations: whether he did it or not (and he has always emphatically denied the accusations and never tested positive), pretty well everyone else was at it, those were the times he lived in, and his achievements were immense by any standards, never mind by those of a man who had recovered from a near-fatal brush with cancer.

But it is not quite as simple as that. Doping was not outlawed in Anquetil's time; he was breaking no rules. Since the death of Tom Simpson in 1967, attitudes have changed and hardened, particularly since the introduction of sophisticated doping products whose long-term effects could only be guessed at.

The isolated death of a man fuddled with amphetamine and alcohol and over-exerting himself in furnace-like conditions on the exposed slopes of the Mont Ventoux was one thing. A group of young riders dying in their sleep 20 years ago, their hearts no longer able to pump their artificially thickened blood through their veins, is quite another. Tolerance of the old ways belongs to the old days; it has no place in the present, and a serial offender such as Riccardo Ricco is held in general contempt. Nor, despite the remarkable story of his recovery from surgery to brain, lungs and testicles, did Armstrong's behaviour encourage the sort of sympathy so freely granted to Anquetil and the men with whom he raced. The Texan's persecution of those who campaigned against doping is a permanent stain on his reputation. "Don't spit in the soup" is a motto that has long outlived any conceivable justification.

The announcement of the dropping of the case against Armstrong came from the US Attorney's office in Los Angeles, and reminded us that its primary purpose was not to prove that the rider had doped. In the US, sports-related doping is not a federal crime. The effect of doping is the issue, and in Armstrong's case an attempt was being made to discover if sponsorship money provided by a US government body had been used to subsidise a doping programme by his US Postal team. Fraudulent misuse of federal funds would have been the crime, rather than cheating in order to distort competition.

The appointment as lead investigator of Jeff Novitsky, who cracked the Balco case involving Marion Jones and investigated the baseball stars Barry Bonds and Roger Clemens, suggested that the truth, whatever it was, would finally be established. No one expected 20 months of work to be abandoned so suddenly and – to many eyes – inconclusively, with Novitsky's office apparently still in the process of setting up appointments for further interviews.

The decision seems to have been made on a cost-benefit basis. Even with testimony from such former team-mates as Floyd Landis, himself stripped of a title for drug use, and Tyler Hamilton, both of whom told Novitsky they had seen Armstrong doping, a court hearing would have been lengthy and expensive for the government and its outcome uncertain. Why spend all that money on an effort to bring down a national hero, particularly one whose own legal armoury is equally well stocked?

It would have been nice to have established the truth, either way, and put it beyond dispute. A suggestion that the US Anti-Drug Agency will continue the pursuit seems unrealistic. Novitsky had the resources but could not find the incontrovertible evidence that went beyond a matter of one man's word against another's (or, in the case of Emma O'Reilly, the former US Postal masseuse who told her story to David Walsh and Pierre Ballester, the authors of *LA Confidential*, one woman's word).

Case closed, then. There will never be a smoking gun, or a dripping syringe. We are left to examine our own conclusions, and to wonder how it really feels to be Lance Armstrong.

CONTADOR VOWS TO FIGHT ON OVER DRUGS BAN AS PENALTIES MOUNT

The Guardian, 8 February 2012

Alberto Contador is considering appealing against the two-year ban he was handed by the Court of Arbitration for Sport (Cas) for failing a dope test during his victorious 2010 Tour de France campaign.

The 29-year-old Spaniard, who was stripped of the Tour title by the Cas in its ruling published on Monday, told a news conference that he was innocent and planned to return to competition when the retroactive ban ends in August.

"My lawyers are examining the possibilities and as I have said before we have to fight to the end," Contador said when asked if he would appeal Lausanne-based Cas's decision in the Swiss federal court, which he must do within 30 days.

"With the sentence in my hand the sensation I still feel is that I am innocent. I did not dope myself. I will continue in cycling. I will continue to do so in a clean way as I have all my life. And I know that will make me stronger in the future."

Contador, who won the Tour in 2007, 2009 and 2010 and is widely regarded as the greatest cyclist of his generation, was speaking at a hotel in his home town of Pinto near Madrid. He tested positive for the banned anabolic agent clenbuterol during the 2010 Tour, claiming the drug got into his system from contaminated meat.

According to cyclingnews.com Contador's doping conviction could cost him over euros 5m (£4.15m) in fees, fines and lost earnings. The Spaniard is waiting for the Cas to rule on the UCI's attempt to fine him euros 2.4m and 70 per cent of his contract. With Contador estimated to be on euros 5m a year with his team Saxo Bank, that could mean an additional euros 3.5m fine. Contador is also set to lose all the prize money earned after January 25 2011 – including that gained from his win in last year's Giro d'Italia and the 11 other wins since the disciplinary process started – and will not be able to earn money from cycling until his ban expires in August. Andy Schleck of Luxembourg, who finished second to Contador in the 2010 Tour de France, will now be elevated to champion.

TOUR TIMELINE

1 July 1903: The first Tour begins when 60 cyclists set off from Montgeron on the 2,500km, six-stage, 19-day race. Maurice Garin wins and 21 finish.

1904: Henri Desgrange, the founder of the race, fears that the second Tour will be the last with riders being attacked in the long night stages and the use of caffeine pills and cocaine becoming common. Henri Cornet becomes the youngest ever winner of the Tour.

1905: Stages are shortened and Ballon d'Alsace, the first major climb of the event, is added.

1907–8: Lucian Petit-Breton becomes the first cyclist to win twice.

1910: The "Circle of Death", a 203-mile journey over the Peyresourde, Aspin, Tourmalet and Aubisque peaks in the Pyrenees, is added.

1919: The *maillot jaune*, yellow jersey, is introduced to identify the overall leader (chosen because *L'Auto*, sponsor of the race, is produced on yellow paper)

1924: The first drug revelations with the Pélissier brothers, Henri and Francis, admitting to using chloroform, cocaine, asprin and "horse ointment".

1930: Henri Desgrange decides to bring national teams to the Tour – previously sponsored by bicycle manufacturers. Also, introduces the publicity caravan.

1935: Spain's Francesco Cepeda dies after a crash on the descent from the Galibier pass.

1937: Desgrange agrees to the use of three-speed derailleurs.

1947: The Tour returns after the Second World War. Jacques Goddet of *L'Équipe* takes over as director.

1951: The Mont Ventoux climb is added to the Tour.

1953: The 50th anniversary is won by Louison Bobet, the first of his three consecutive wins.

1955: A British team competes for the first time.

1958: A Tour official is killed after a collision with a competitor.

1961: The return to sponsored teams is announced.

1962: Tom Simpson becomes the first British rider to wear the yellow jersey.

1966: Drug tests are introduced. Tour cyclists go on strike at the way they are being handled.

1967: British rider Tom Simpson dies on Mont Ventoux.

1975: The Tour ends on the Champs-Élysées for the first time.

1975: Eddy Merckx is punched by a spectator.

1978: Michel Pollentier of Belgium wins the stage at l'Alpe d'Huez but when he is dope tested afterwards the doctors find an elaborate system of tubes running from his armpit to his penis containing clean urine. He is disqualified.

1978: Bernard Hinault wins the first of five Tours.

1981: Jacques Boyers becomes the first American to take part in the race.

1984: A women's race, the Tour Féminin, is introduced.

1984: Scotsman Robert Millar wins the mountain grand prix – the first Briton to win outright the red polka dot jersey as King of the Mountain.

1986: Greg LeMond is the first American, and non-European, to win the race.

1988: The entire race goes on a 10-minute strike in protest against a drugs test on Pedro Delgado.

1989: Having recovered from an accidental gunshot wound, LeMond wins the closest Tour ever, beating France's Laurent Fignon by eight seconds on the Champs-Élysées finish.

1991: Miguel Indurain wins the Tour, the first of five consecutive victories.

1993: Lance Armstrong competes in his first Tour de France.

1994: British cyclist Chris Boardman records the fastest

Pro-logue stage time, reaching 55.152kph over a 7.2km stretch.

1995: Fabio Casartelli falls to his death on a bend going down the Col de Portet d'Aspet.

1997: Uzbekistan's Djamolidine Abdoujaparov, the "Tashkent Terror", becomes the first rider disqualified for taking banned substances.

1998: The Festina cycling team is expelled in the first week of the Tour following allegations of drug use. Richard Virenque, seven times the winner of King of the Mountains, is part of the team and makes a tearful confession.

1999: Cancer survivor Lance Armstrong wins the race, the first American to do so since Greg LeMond.

2003: The centenary Tour starts from Montgeron, the starting point of the first race.

2005: Lance Armstrong wins his seventh Tour.

2006: The start of "Operation Puerto", a Spanish blood-doping inquiry.

2007: The Tour starts in Britain.

2011: British cyclist Mark Cavendish becomes the first Briton to win the green jersey.

2011: Australian cyclist Cadel Evans wins the Tour at the age of 34 (the oldest winner was 36-year-old Firmin Lambot in 1922).

2012: Alberto Contador is banned for two years for doping and is stripped of his 2010 Tour de France victory.

INDEX